A Month of Sundays

A Month of Sundays

Books One and Two

David Thatcher Wilson

Writers Club Press
New York Lincoln Shanghai

A Month of Sundays
Books One and Two

Writers Club Press
an imprint of iUniverse, Inc.

For information address:
iUniverse, Inc.
2021 Pine Lake Road, Suite 100
Lincoln, NE 68512
www.iuniverse.com

ISBN: 0-595-25829-8

Printed in the United States of America

One man cannot do right in one department of life whilst he is occupied in doing wrong in any other department. Life is one indivisible whole.

—Gandhi

Contents

Preface

The genesis of Sunday Musings really isn't important. Suffice it to say that it is a message that gets e.mailed and faxed to over 200 addressees each Sunday that I'm able. [Of course, many of those are my university students who probably are afraid to ask to be removed from distribution.] Be that as it may, there have been enough requests for a compilation of past Sunday Musings that I decided to go ahead with its preparation. I would like to thank my students at Trinity International University who were the most vocal in requesting this book. I hope that they did so even recognizing that it would not affect their grades one way or the other.

But my greatest most heart-felt appreciation goes to my Lord who gave me the ability to sometimes see things differently than others, and the skill (I hope) to be able to express in writing what I have perceived with my eyes and my spirit.

Introduction

This is not a book to sit with and read for an hour or two. Rather, I hope that it is a pool into which you can dip for an occasional drink. The drink may be refreshing. It may be stimulating. It may be calming. But whatever else, it should be challenging. The following **Sunday Musings** will ask you to think…to consider yourself and the world in which you live…and to pray.

Book One

Sunday Musings
1

Beloved,

One or two evenings a week I drive about thirty miles south to teach some university courses. Driving down the Florida Turnpike one summer night I was totally blown away by the brilliant sunset. It was breathtaking. Florida is quite flat, so there's lots of sky for the sunset to utilize. Out west the sun was behind a mass of clouds. They were dense enough to keep the sun from shining through, but the edges of the cloud fairly gleamed with a fiery golden luminescence. Overhead the clouds weren't just gray or pink, they were shades of lilac and mauve and dusty rose. The sky blended from rich azure to a bleeding crimson. And I thought to myself, *How can anyone witness this magnificence and not believe in God?*

I guess the more scientifically minded would tell me that the reds were only the result of the angle of the sun—because it was low in the sky its light had to travel through more atmosphere and the colors were just the result of refraction from dust in the air. And the clouds, well, they are just water vapor and ice crystals formed by the normal evaporation of water and other atmospheric conditions. It's not all that mysterious and artistic. It's easily and naturally explained. Right! And the Mona Lisa is just an amalgam of natural pigments mixed with oils spread on a substrate of natural fibers spun and woven into a planar surface stretched on a wooden frame. No artist. No creativity. No genius—just a natural happenstance. Believe that and I've got some "waterfront" property in the Everglades to sell you.

Have you ever spent a lot of time searching for just that one unique gift for someone special? You traveled and searched and looked, hoping to find something super exceptional just for that one particular and precious individual. You couldn't wait to see the look on their face when they saw that gift that was selected "just for them." You've done that, haven't you?

Well, God is painting these sunsets JUST FOR YOU. He can't wait to see the look on YOUR face as you see the gift that He has made JUST FOR YOU. Did you smile? Did you thank Him? Think about it.

Blessings!

Sunday Musings
2

Beloved,

> On the street, I saw a small girl, cold and shivering in a thin dress, with little hope of a decent meal. I became angry and said to God:
>
> "Lord, why did You permit this? Why don't You do something about it?"
>
> For a while God said nothing. That night He replied quite suddenly: "I certainly did do something about it…I made YOU."

When we drive around Miami or Ft. Lauderdale or your city, and see the homeless sleeping in doorways or under highway overpasses, do we think, *Why doesn't* someone *do something about them?* When we see trash on the side of the road, do we think, *Gosh, what a bunch of slobs people are! Why doesn't* someone *pick that up?* When we read in the news about a family burned out of their home, all of their belongings destroyed, do we think, *I sure hope* someone *takes care of them.* When we hear about another "adult" bookstore being built; or another abortion clinic being opened; or another corrupt politician being indicted; or another child being hospitalized as a victim of abuse; or another elderly person being found, days or weeks after having died alone, uncared for by anyone…when we hear of these do we think, Someone *should do something?*

An old hymn goes, "I am the church, you are the church, we are the church together." It means that the church, the Body of Christ, is not made up of *other* people. It's made up of us. It was the same when I was active in the Sierra Club. Then we used to point out to members that *we* were the Sierra Club, not someone else, and if *we* didn't do something, then there was no one else to get things done.

In America we are so used to getting *someone else* to do things. At the Lutheran school that I used to administer, parents of students were required to volunteer 15 hours of service during the school year. Or they could pay $10 an hour to "buy" their way out, and thereby get *someone else* to do the work for them. Well, yes, we did get some parent volunteers, but we got an awful lot who were anxious to pay to get *someone else* to do it for them.

How about you? Do you take responsibility, or do you look to point at someone else? You know, when we are pointing at *someone else* to volunteer them to do something, we've got three fingers pointing back at *us*. Why do you think God designed our hand to do that?

Are you dissatisfied, angry, discouraged with, or aggravated by...*something*? **Anything?** Then maybe *YOU* should do something about it. Rather than waiting for *someone else*. Think about it.

Blessings!

Sunday Musings
3

Beloved,

Did you know that **M*A*S*H** is back on cable? I know the plot of every show by heart, but when I've got the time I still enjoy watching. There is one episode when Hawkeye temporarily loses his eyesight through an accident. He spends most of the episode with his eyes bandaged, but comments that with his eyes out of commission, his other senses have become more sensitive, and he "never felt more alive."

How many senses do we have…five? Sight, smell, touch, taste, hearing. Yes, five. Unfortunately, in today's world all five are so constantly bombarded, we are receiving such a continuous amalgam of sensory inputs, that we are dumbfounded. We taste our smells, and see our sounds, and feel…well, we feel overwhelmed by it all. There's so much bombarding us we are not able to take pleasure in our lives…to appreciate what is all around us…to completely feel the joyous sensory inputs we are receiving.

When you drive down the highway, what do you see? Traffic? Trash? Billboards? And too much of it? When I drive down the Ronald Reagan Turnpike to Miami, I don't see a water-filled ditch by the side of the road, with occasional discarded tires and junk littering it. I see a life-filled canal, with delicately flowering water lilies and bog lilies, turtles sunning on the bank, a Great Blue Heron slo-o-owly stalking his lunch. Does that purple house [yes, you northerners, it actually is purple] near the Golden Glades interchange repel you? Ignore it. Marvel instead at the massive Banyan tree in the front yard. Object to hearing the booming bass from the kids' cars, or the diesels on the highway? Listen for the squawk of the parrots, the laughing of the gulls, the scolding blue jays, the rhapsody of the mockingbird. When the tide is low, you can either turn up your nose at the smell of the black sand, or you can recognize and appreciate the rich aroma of life and death of a marsh.

One of the things that Hawkeye spoke of was *listening* to a rainstorm. I've done that. Have you? No, you can't hear it over the sound of the television or the stereo. When the wind is blowing, do you listen to its wailing, or do you close the curtains to help close out the NOISE? It was a number of years ago that I was at my mother-in-law's for Christmas, at her home on top of a New Jersey mountain, and went out for a walk. No, on my crutches I can't walk far, but I went a little ways, and then stood in the dark and the cold and listened to the soft whisper of the snow coming down. And the occasional rustle of…something…in the woods. Robert Frost: *The only other sound's the swish of easy wind and downy flake.*

What's keeping you from enjoying what surrounds us? Do you think you're too important? Too busy? Too stressed? Camel dung! We *have* to take the time to value what the Lord has given us. HE doesn't want to hear that we didn't have time to appreciate what He went to so much trouble to create. Just for our pleasure. Did you see Robin Williams in "The Dead Poets' Society?" *Carpe Diem! Seize the day!* Take the time to appreciate what we have. Not satisfied with what you have? You'd better be. Which ridiculously wealthy man was it who, when asked how much money was enough answered, "Just a little more?" *If you are not happy with what you have, you'll never be satisfied with what you get.* You can strive to achieve more yet be happy with what you have. It's where you set your priorities.

After almost dying in the accident that left me a paraplegic, I've realized that I am so blessed by what the Lord has given me. Sure, there are a few things I'd like to have. Maybe I'll get them, someday. Perhaps not. But like the little sign Chris once gave me says:

THE BEST THINGS IN LIFE ARE NOT THINGS.
SEEK YE FIRST THE KINGDOM OF GOD.

You can't take "things" with you. Hopefully you've already stored up treasure in the Kingdom of God. Think about it.

Blessings!

Sunday Musings
4

Beloved,

♫ Rainy days and Mondays always get me down. ♫
—*The Carpenters*

Yawn! It's Monday morning. We've got the entire workweek stretched out in front of us. Are you looking forward to it, or are you kind of *blah* about the whole thing? Same old job...same old workplace...same old tasks to perform. "Same-old, same-old." Is what you do for a living getting...boring? Are you finding it harder and harder to get excited by your work? Is it beginning to show *in* your work?

How would you feel if, tomorrow morning, your phone should ring, and when you answer it you find it is an acquaintance that you respect, and he says to you:

> *Don't say anything, just listen:*
> *I just wanted to call and tell you how very much your friendship means to me. I know that we don't see each other a lot, or get to talk very often, but I think about you a lot, and you have made a big difference in my life. I appreciate you. So, I should have told you this before, and I'm glad I'm finally telling you now. Have a great week. I love you.*

And he hangs up the phone.

How does your week look now? Do things look a little less "same-old, same-old?" Do you think that you'll be able to do your job a little better? With more enthusiasm? And joy?

Why? Why the change? It was simply because someone, someone you respect, called and said some encouraging and uplifting words to you. It's just as simple as that—and as profound. Is there someone who could benefit from such a phone call *from you*? You know, when you make that phone call you benefit from it, too. Gives you a warm fuzzy feeling. Try it! And thanks to Zig Ziglar for the idea.

Remember: God loves you…whether you want Him to or not.

Blessings!

Sunday Musings
5

Beloved,

The Clinton presidency caused a lot of hard feelings. Was what he did a criminal offense? I don't know, and I don't care, any more. What I'm more concerned with is our country's apparent nonchalance with illicit sexual behavior. During the media frenzy of that time an editorial cartoon reminded us how scandalized we were when President Carter admitted that he had sinned when he had "lusted in his heart." Do you remember that? Poor Jimmy was pilloried! And Gary Hart had to pull out of his presidential race when he was photographed with a woman-not-his-wife on his lap. Clinton first lied under oath, and then *admitted* to [what most of us would call] actually committing illicit extra-marital sexual acts…and, if the polls are true, the majority of Americans sloughed it off. "It's just sex. No big deal." No big deal indeed!

What on earth has happened to our national moral values? Have we honestly decided that, since we have a "jingle in our jeans," we'll let pass moral and ethical violations? Degeneracy? Bill Bennett, in his book *The Death of Outrage*, reminds us that in the 1996 election the voters stated, "character doesn't count." It seemed that as long as we were making money, then nothing else mattered. This was the "modern" view of life.

So, where are we now? Our enlightened American society has "advanced" to where we have a President admitting to lying to us, but because it was *only* about cheating on his wife, then we don't care. That's private. We've "advanced" to where we have to shoo children from the room before the evening news comes on, because they are going to openly discuss things that "little ears" shouldn't hear. We have "advanced" to where the doctrine of separation of church and state, *a doctrine that is not stated in the Constitution*, is used to ensure that virtually anything goes in schools…EXCEPT Judeo/Christian morality and mores. We've "advanced" to where, if we can re-define simple words to satisfy our own desires, we can excuse virtually any behavior. We've "advanced" to where television and movie producers revel in "pushing the envelope," trying to expand what we will accept, rather than giving us what we truly want. We've "advanced" to where a state governor has to threaten to call out the National Guard to keep the Ten Commandments on a courtroom wall because higher courts have said that such behavior is tantamount to the state endorsing religion.

Aren't we proud of how far we have "advanced" our society? No more being confined by those old-fashioned moral principles of the past. No more being inhibited by such outmoded beliefs like honor, truthfulness, fidelity, loyalty, and the like. No more having to live by those archaic tenets of Judeo-Christianity. We're modern. Anything goes.

George Washington once said, "It is impossible to rightly govern the world without God and the Bible." Billy Graham said that if God doesn't bring judgment upon America, then He owes an apology to Sodom and Gomorrah. What do you say? Think about it.

Blessings!

Sunday Musings
6

Beloved,

> 1 Kings 19:11 ...*and a great and strong wind tore the mountains, and broke the rocks in pieces before the LORD. But the LORD was not in the wind.*

I think that it is a Chinese a curse, "May you live in interesting times." It brings to mind the week in south Florida we prepared and waited for a visit from Hurricane Georges. We put up our storm shutters, took our patio furniture and grills indoors, and stocked up on bottled water and canned food and batteries. We backed up our computers and put the tapes and disks in waterproof containers. We made certain that our insurance policies were protected but readily available...just in case. Even many of us who didn't expect a serious hit took the time to prepare—and to pray, of course. There's no sense in being stupid about these things. Fortunately, here in Broward County Georges visited us with his winds, but not with his real fury. In the Keys they spoke of him as "Furious Georges" but here, in Ft. Lauderdale, damage was minimal.

The preparation was good practice, though. Those of us, who were here for the visit of Hurricane Andrew, back in '92, were a little more serious about getting ready this time. In the New Testament Andrew brought Peter to Jesus. In south Florida, Andrew brought a lot of us to a fuller understanding of hurricane preparation.

It's kind of funny, though. We all knew that Georges was out there, but watching him on the Weather Channel it was a good guess that he wouldn't hit the Ft. Lauderdale area. Sure, we'd get some heavy weather, but it wasn't likely that we'd actually get a *hurricane* over us. Nonetheless, the populace raced about laying in food supplies, buying up all of the plywood in sight, taking down their mailboxes (they can become missiles in a high wind), and generally getting real prepared...for something that might not even happen. The reason it's "funny" is that there is one thing that most definitely IS going to happen, and so many aren't bothering to prepare at all. We spend every waking hour thinking about anything *but* that inevitability. *Maybe if we don't pay attention, it won't actually happen.*

Of course you know what I am talking about: The end of all of this. The Biblical end of the world. Do you profess to be a Christian? Then you expect Jesus to return. Maybe not this week, but He will return. Are you Jewish? Then it might not be Yeshua you are expecting, but you, too, await the Savior. Right? There's a bumper sticker about

JESUS IS COMING, AND HE IS TICKED OFF!

At whom? You? Me? Or is it at someone else?

It's a shame. Andrew brought Peter to Jesus. Hurricane Andrew brought a lot of people to the realization of their mortality. But so many more just don't see...or don't care. Well, one of these days it will not be the roar of the wind, but the blowing of trumpets and the *shofar*, and then "a still, small voice." We're prepared for the hurricane. We're prepared for the blizzard. We're ready for the earth's anger. Are we prepared for **HIS**? Think about it.

Blessings!

Sunday Musings
7

Beloved,

Maybe something good came out of the moral/ethical/political mess in our nation's capital in the decade of the 1990's. It's conceivable that we Americans finally began to see where the self-indulgence of the so-called "Me Generation" has gotten us.

Unfortunately, my generation, reared as we were in the swinging '60's, has confused ***freedom*** with ***license***. Rather than using the glorious liberty granted to us by living in the United States of America, we have abused it, and the courts continually ratify our egocentrism. Accordingly, through our court-approved misbehavior, we do as we please, even if that is against the popular norms of our parents. Indeed, we usually go out of our way to refute the beliefs of our parents as stodgy and out of touch with reality. In our liberal colleges we learned "situation ethics." Our motto was, "If it feels good, do it," and do it we did. There were no holds barred…nothing taboo…nothing sacred. There were no such things as "absolutes." Relativism was everything. Look where it has gotten us now.

Through the liberal courts and media and educational institutions we have been led to believe that there are such things as "victim-less crimes." "Who does prostitution *really* hurt?" "If I want to take drugs, so what if it ruins my health? It's *my* body." "Sure President Clinton had a sexual affair and lied about it, but why should the nation be worried or upset about that? It was just 'recreational sex,' and he only lied [albeit under oath] to keep from hurting his wife and daughter."

He only lied to keep from hurting his wife and daughter. Did anyone ever think that maybe he could have restrained himself from illicit sex to keep from hurting his family? But that's not the way we think, any more. My generation has run frantically away from Biblical self-denial and toward [supposedly] no-fault self-gratification until our norms, our beliefs, our **absolutes** just aren't there anymore.

Well, God willing, the furor, which arose over Clinton's illicit liaison, the hurt that it caused his family, and beyond that the agony which it caused the country and the world, will shock us back to our senses. Maybe we will now realize that a little "victimless" crime, in this case sexual and ethical, can actually have effects far beyond our imaginations. Perhaps we will finally be brought to realize that there **are** absolute truths, by which moral human beings must live. Son of a gun! Maybe there is something to those old, antiquated Ten Commandment-things. Maybe when we say, "One nation, *under God...*" it means that Someone actually is watching. Maybe it means that the beliefs that our founders espoused over two-hundred years ago aren't out-of-date but can apply to modern life. "Ya think?" I do. You think about it.

Blessings!

Sunday Musings
8

Beloved,

Did you hear about the pastor who was asked to perform a funeral, but didn't have a dark suit? He didn't have much money, either, so he went to the local pawnshop to see if he could get a good deal. To his surprise, the pawnbroker had a solid black suit, just his size, in very good shape, and very cheap. He was so pleased! As he was paying for the suit he asked the pawnbroker how he could possibly afford to sell suits so inexpensively. The pawnbroker grinned and admitted that all of his suits had been sold to him by the local funeral parlor. They would use the suits for the viewings, and then remove them before the body was interred. The pastor felt a little strange wearing a suit that had last been worn by a corpse, but since no one else would know, and he couldn't afford a new suit any other way, why not?

Everything at the funeral went fine until, in the middle of his sermon, the minister casually started to stick his hand into his pants pocket...only to find that there were no pockets! There he was preaching about the importance of living in light of eternity today, as he himself wore a pair of pants without pockets that had been last worn by a corpse.

Are you spending too much time *[Mt 6:19] lay[ing] up treasures on earth for yourselves, where moth and rust corrupt, and where thieves break through and steal?* Can you not be content with what you have? You know, you can't take it with you.

A sense of contentment is not something with which we Americans are born. We have to learn it, and unfortunately our televisions and magazines and radios—all of the advertisers—keep telling us that we need **MORE**. Buy! Consume! Obtain! Acquire! We are taught that in school, too. More is better. Strive to be #1 in everything. Achieve! Advance! Attain! You aren't a success unless you can proceed further and faster than all others. Have you ever caught yourself looking enviably at the other guy's car…condo…career? Have you ever lain awake at night trying to figure out how you can get yourself into position for that promotion, pay raise, pat-on-the-back before your co-worker beats you to it? Where do your priorities lie?

A Greek sage once said: "To whom little is not enough, nothing is enough." But I kind of prefer the way that the Bible puts it in 1 Timothy 6-7: *For we brought nothing into the world, and it is clear that we can carry nothing out.* You can't take it with you. You can leave it behind. But, then, what is that? Wouldn't it be far better to leave behind the love and memories that *your* contentment could produce in those who love you and whom you love? What's important to you? Where are your priorities? When you leave this world, your pockets will be empty. Will your memory be empty, too? Think about it.

Blessings!

Sunday Musings
9

Beloved,

Some time ago, in the national weekly edition of *THE WASHING-TON TIMES*, there was an article about the decreasing readiness of our military forces. Statistics showed that the four major branches of the military discharged nearly 36% of the people who enlisted in 1993 before they finished their four-year commitments. An analyst stated, "It doesn't mean they don't have values, but it means a large number of them have values that are pretty largely removed from what tradition has considered our values." The article was concerned about the readiness of the military, but it makes me think about values.

What a strange statement: "It doesn't mean they don't have values..." just that their values aren't congruent with those of society at large. I looked up *value* in my *Webster's New Collegiate*: "relative worth, utility or importance: degree of excellence...something intrinsically valuable or desirable." I guess that means that *values* are what a person or society considers valuable. So when almost 36% of enlistees are being kicked out of the military for "misbehavior, performance shortfalls, obesity, pregnancy and physical problems," it means that they just can't reconcile *their* belief system with that of the military. Believe me, when I was at Ft. Dix in basic training, I knew that the Army was bigger than me, and that I'd better play by their rules. That's not the way it is today. Today the individual's values are more important (to them) than society's.

Where do we learn our values? At school, of course, but I would postulate that mostly we learn our values at home. So, if the values of these young soldiers and sailors are manifesting are not "ours," WHY NOT? Who taught them what they are acting out?

Unfortunately, too many of us have abrogated our parental responsibility of teaching moral values. We have succumbed to the belief that our children should not be hindered in their personal growth by the imposition of *our* moral values on them. They should be allowed to learn for themselves. Let nature take its course. Allow their own human personalities the freedom to develop as they will. We've let them "do their own thing," even in school, where teachers have been constrained from applying correction or discipline for fear it would "hinder" the unchecked development of the child. We have wanted our children to be free to express their "inner selves."

Well, they've expressed it. Man is not an intrinsically moral and ethical being—especially when a child. Children are the epitome of egocentrism. They truly believe that the world should revolve about them, and when we have not had the courage or wisdom to show them the limits by which they must live to be a part of human society, we have no one to blame but ourselves.

Do you have children that you are raising, or grandchildren that can still be influenced by your values? Are you doing anything about it? Think about it.

Blessings!

Sunday Musings
10

Beloved,

Oh wad some power the giftie gie us to see oursels as others see us.
—Robert Burns

I went to a funeral some time ago. I didn't know the lady. She was the grandmother of a friend/employee. As I sat with the family and heard them talk about "Gram," and as I listened to the Pastor deliver his eulogy, I couldn't help but think of the difference between the two people remembered. Not that there were glaring discrepancies. Not at all. What struck me was the dichotomy that one's perspective provides, and it got me to thinking about how I have always viewed my parents—as parents, as Mom and Dad—while others viewed them as acquaintances or friends—as Dot and Bud. You know, it was fascinating. And frustrating! I always knew that they were kind, giving, and interesting people. Why, then, did it take me until they were gone to realize that they had roles other than Mom and Dad? No, come on, give me a break—I'm not that dumb! Of course I *realized* it, but I never, ever, took the time to look at them outside their parental roles. I never took the time to fully appreciate them as friends...interesting personalities...individuals outside their parental capacity. Have you done that with your parents? Or grandparents? Or other elderly acquaintances? It is so darn easy to catalog people...to categorize them...to slot them into a given characterization, and then not bother to delve any more deeply into their beings. To discover their true natures. To savor their uniqueness.

My mother was always fascinated. No, that is a complete thought. She was not just fascinated by a given thing. Mom was fascinated by EVERYTHING. She wanted to see everything, to do everything, to know how everything worked, to know why everything was done. It all just fascinated her. As her son, this was always just a somewhat cute quirky personality trait that was embarrassing during my know-it-all teen years. Man, I wish that I had stepped back, really looked at Dorothy, and appreciated this facet of her. The picture of Mom that I have on my desk is one where she is peering through a kaleidoscope. She loved them. And Dad was so interesting, too: A veteran of the war in the Pacific, a sales executive, a world traveler, a knowledgeable seaman, and an excellent and accomplished handyman. Furniture building and refinishing, chair caning, jewelry making. He was so multi-faceted. I just never took full advantage of knowing either of them.

Are your parents and/or grandparents still alive? Do you really know them…as individuals…as people? Have you ever forced yourself out of *your* role as child or grandchild, and looked at them with the eyes of others? Try it. DO IT! Enjoy it. You may be surprised and pleased and enriched by whom you find.

And, Mom and Dad—I'm sorry it took so long. I sure do miss you.

Blessings!

Sunday Musings
11

Beloved,

It must have been almost thirty years ago. Chris and I bought a book for my father's birthday from a Barnes & Noble discount catalog that sold remaindered books. It was a big tome on ship construction. When Dad got it, he felt that it was too technical for him to enjoy, so he took it back to a Barnes & Noble store in New York City. They (and he) didn't realize that the book had been sold at a deep discount, so they refunded him the full cover price, and he called me up to scold me for spending so much money. When I told him how much I had actually spent, he returned to Barnes & Noble and insisted that they take back the money that they had over-refunded him. They didn't know any better, *but Dad did.* He knew that he had received money that wasn't truly his, and there was no question but that he return it. Dad had integrity.

Have you ever received too much change when you've been in line at the grocery store? What did you do? Did you just put it in your pocket, and congratulate yourself on "putting something over" on the store? Whose money was it, honestly? The store's. Whose pocket was it in? Yours. Was that integrity?

What is integrity? *Integrity is what you do when no one is looking.* It's doing the right thing just because it is right. Not because someone is looking. Not because it might get you an award. Or reward. Or a pat on the back. Just because it is the right thing to do.

We used to believe in integrity. We used to believe in absolutes…right and wrong. Black and white. Now we seem to believe in shades of gray. When I was in college, in the '60's, they taught us "situation ethics." There are no such things as "absolutes." If it feels good, do it. If you don't harm anyone else, then it is OK. That was great for college kids who wanted to "get away with things," but is it all right for a way of life for an adult? For a community? For a country?

There's a further part of this. Biblically, an unforgivable sinner is one who sins in order to repent, and who then sins afresh in order to repent again. "If a man has an unclean thing in his hands, he may wash them in all the seas of the world, and he will never be clean; but if he throws the unclean thing away, a little water will suffice." Integrity also means admitting your mistakes, *and refraining from doing them again.* Seems kind of logical, doesn't it? Didn't we used to say, "A wise man learns from his mistakes?" Now, though, it seems as though apologizing wipes the slate clean, and gives us license to go ahead and do it again.

As much as it might crimp what we *want* to do, there *is* an absolute Right. There *is* an absolute Wrong. And we choose between the two at our own peril. John Bunyan once heard a voice that asked him: "Wilt thou leave thy sins and go to heaven, or wilt thou have thy sins and go to hell?"

Which "wilt thou have?" Think about it.

Blessings!

Sunday Musings
12

Beloved,

At my regular Friday morning breakfast with a bunch of like-minded brothers we were asked to pray for an 8-year old girl named Missy. Missy was at a gymnastics competition out-of-state when something went wrong. I don't know if she missed a vault or a dismount, but whatever happened Missy landed on her head. She was in a coma, on a respirator, with intra-cranial bleeding. We prayed hard for her.

Whenever I hear of something tragic like this my initial reaction is "Why?" Why did this happen to a child? Lots of people take it further: "Why did God allow (or cause) this to happen?" It is such an age-old question—Why do bad things happen to good people? Heck, I've had people ask that about my accident. Why did it happen? And then people like to shake their fists and rail against "the fates," or "destiny," or God.

The thing is: stuff happens. God doesn't *cause* it to happen. He may *allow* it to happen, but we are given free will, and with this gift comes the ability to cause things to happen and allow things to happen. So, stuff happens.

Then, too, Nietzsche said: "That which doesn't kill us makes us stronger." That can seem kind of glib, when we are the ones suffering. And, too, there are times when that well-meaning Christian friend comes up to us and quotes Romans: *And we know that all things work together for good to those who love God, to those who are called according to His purpose.* I truly believe that, but when you are lying there, in my case paralyzed from the neck down, not sure what has happened and what is happening to you, that's not necessarily what you need to hear at that precise moment.

But, ultimately, stuff does happen. We have to accept that as a given, then go on from there. Prayer does help. Worry does not. We have to learn to pray for others, pray for ourselves, solicit others' prayers for us, and in the end, don't sweat the small stuff. And in the greatest scheme of things, with the exception of our eternal souls…it's *all* small stuff. Think about it.

Blessings!

Sunday Musings
13

Beloved,

This is not a political letter, but during the 2000 election there was a great hoopla in the press about George Bush's answer to the question about what philosopher or great thinker he felt was most important or influential? His answer—"Jesus Christ." Well, as you can imagine the media flipped out. They couldn't quite figure out what to do about it. *Jesus Christ!* What an answer. They figured it was just another example of Bush not knowing about people like DeTocqueville or Kirkegaard. They just could not comprehend the totality of immersion, of focus, of centrality of a life saved by Christ. Even Gary Bauer didn't seem to get it. He commented about Jesus Christ changing the world (which, of course, He did), but he seemed to miss the personal relationship that is so much the part of the evangelical Christian experience.

Cokie Roberts, on one morning news program, tried hard not to denigrate Jesus, but wondered what this "great thinker" would have to do with third world debt and other modern problems. George Will commented about Gospel meaning "the good news," and some Christian traditions believed that talking about this news was what they were supposed to do (closer), but that *his* tradition was to be more private about his religion (is he embarrassed by his beliefs?).

I guess what amazed, and somewhat discouraged, me was the total lack of understanding of what it is to be a born again believer who walks with Christ every day, who tries to use Biblical teachings to guide his every action and decision. I'm sure they have heard of the **WWJD** movement. **W**hat **W**ould **J**esus **D**o? But I guess to them it is just a sort of nice thought…not a way of life. They obviously don't understand the Great Commission of Matthew 28, where Jesus, Himself, tells us to *Go therefore and make disciples of all the nation…teaching them to observe all things that I have commanded you.* They don't realize that the teachings of the Bible (the WHOLE Bible), and especially the teachings of Jesus Christ *are* fully applicable to all of today's problems, if they would just read them.

So, for those of you who don't understand what I am talking about, that's OK. We evangelicals don't think that we are better than anyone else. As the bumper sticker says,

I'M NOT PERFECT, JUST SAVED.

And remember the other bumper sticker that says:

God loves you, whether you want Him to or not.

Think about it.

Blessings!

Sunday Musings
14

Beloved,

A friend asked me to pray for a 17-year old boy. He was a passenger in a serious auto accident. When they opened him up in emergency surgery, they found that his aorta had ruptured! They had to clamp it off as they worked on him, and the loss of blood to his spinal cord has left him a paraplegic.

That's about how old my son was when I had my accident that left me a paraplegic. I've always said that it was "better me than Jonathan," since he was so young and I was already 45. Now there's this young boy, paralyzed from the chest down. My friend has said that she might want me to go up and visit with him…if he regains consciousness. Of course I'll go. I'll try to help him see that this is not the end of his world, but it is the end of his world as he knew it for 17 years.

You can never tell how someone will react when they find themselves in this sort of situation. I've been thinking about that a fair amount recently. When something like this happens, it creates a "new reality" for an individual. You do have your memories, your yesterdays; but your "now" world changes. Now you have to decide whether you are going to strive against the fates, or accept your life, as modified, and persevere.

In a greater or lesser sense, this is a question that pertains to all of us. We all have changes in our lives. Though when observed dispassionately these changes may, for the most part, seem less drastic than paralysis, when observed from the point of the recipient, or victim, they are every bit as devastating. The death of a beloved pet—or a beloved parent. Breaking a precious piece of china—or a precious leg. Crashing your computer—or your car. *Your* problem *is* the *most difficult in the world* while *you* have to deal with it. How will you deal with it? I guess the answer to that is closely tied up with character, and belief, and spirituality, and strength…

I have one friend, a former boss, actually, who told me that he considered me a hero for how I dealt with my accident. But, no, I have to go along with what Chuck Colson said: "A hero is someone who does what he doesn't have to do." I only did what I had to do.

Do you have problems? What do *you* have to do? The choice is yours. You can beat your breast, shake your fist at the heavens, and cry out, "Why me?" Or you can say, "Well, here's where I am. Here's what I've got. What do I do now?" Oh! And if you want to do it right—PRAY!

Blessings!

Sunday Musings
15

Beloved,

"What if...?" Who hasn't asked that question? What if...I had done things a different way? "What if...?" What if I hadn't gone for that dive trip that landed me as a paraplegic? What would I be doing now? Where would we be? "What if...?"

A movie came out, some time ago, which was about a young man, blind from infancy, who got his sight back through surgery. Apparently, much of the story premise was how he coped with this "new" sense. Fascinating story concept.

I've spent some mind-wandering time attempting to imagine what it would be like to SEE for the first time, or HEAR for the first time. Think of how overwhelming the sensation would be to first hear the 1812 Overture, or the Hallelujah Chorus after of lifetime of silence! Think of how vastly overpowering would be the sensation of first seeing the pinks and reds and purples of a sunset after a lifetime of darkness! On a somewhat smaller scale, I've also tried to consider what it would be like for me...to suddenly be healed. How would I handle it? Would I start walking and running, again? Would I learn to dance? Would I...well, what would I do? "What if...?"

Do you have something that is holding you back? What would you do if that "something" was taken away? Would you actually <u>do</u> things differently? Or would you be lost, now that your crutch (figuratively speaking) was taken away? That takes a little thinking. I like to joke about myself being an "old, fat, cripple," but that's said tongue-in-cheek. I try hard to ignore my disability and do things anyway. The real challenge for you, and me, is to live in *our reality*. No, don't become complacent, but recognize what your reality is.

There is a song by Ian & Sylvia, '60's folk singers, about a man with "a satisfied mind." "The wealthiest man is a pauper at times, compared with the man with a satisfied man." In the New Testament Paul talks about his "thorn in the flesh." Three times he asked the Lord to take it away,

> *But He said to me, 'My grace is sufficient for you, for My power is made perfect in weakness.' Therefore I will boast all the more gladly about my weaknesses, so that Christ's power may rest on me.*

I used to have a little plaque that said, "We can't change the wind, but we can adjust our sails." We can't change our reality, but we can learn to live within it. To cope. To overcome. To succeed. And I'll guarantee you, asking for His help in dealing with our realities is the easiest way to go. Try it.

Blessings!

Sunday Musings
16

Beloved,

> *"Indeed, I tremble for my country when I reflect that God is just."*
> —Thomas Jefferson

Let me ask you: Do you "tremble for [our] country?"

Billy Graham once said that if the Lord does not punish the United States, then He owes an apology to Sodom and Gomorrah. We have become such a coarse and secular society. Do you "tremble for [our] country?"

Princeton University has hired a professor to fill a tenured chair at their Center for Human Values who has stated *in writing* that parents should have the option to kill a disabled baby up to 28 days after its birth. "Killing a disabled infant is not morally equivalent to killing a person. Very often it is not wrong at all." Princeton defends their action in the name of academic freedom. Do you "tremble for [our] country?"

A report in the journal of the American Psychological Association stated that a psychological study showed that child sexual abuse "does not cause intense harm on a pervasive basis," a finding applauded by NAMBLA, the North American Man-Boy Love Association. Pedophilia is psychologically healthy!? Do you "tremble for [our] country?"

In California (of course) a high school valedictorian, who had four years of straight A's behind him, was not allowed to give his prepared address to graduation. He planned to mention "God" and "Jesus Christ" in his speech. We have gotten to the point where, in the name of separation of church and state, we allow everything and anything BUT God. Can you imagine that it is illegal to have the Ten Commandments, the basis of *all* law, displayed in a public courthouse? Do you "tremble for [our] country?"

Do you approve of what is happening in our country? In sales they say, "silence indicates agreement." Do you approve of what is happening in our country? Are you doing anything at all about it? Let me ask you: DO YOU TREMBLE FOR OUR COUNTRY?

> *They came first for the Communists, and I didn't speak up because I wasn't a Communist. Then they came for the Jews, and I didn't speak up because I wasn't a Jew. Then they came for the trade unionists, and I didn't speak up because I was not a trade unionist. Then they came for the Catholics, and I didn't speak up because I was a Protestant. And then they came for me and by that time no one was left to speak up.*
>
> —Rev. Martin Niemoeller,
> a Protestant minister in Nazi Germany, in 1945

God, forgive us, for we know all-to-well what we allow. Think about it.

Blessings!

Sunday Musings
17

Beloved,

I'm sitting here, happily pecking away at my computer...I used to have a manual typewriter. I could understand how it worked. I could see all of the levers and springs. Then I went to an IBM Selectric—fancier, but still reasonably understandable. They just took the old manual one, and put some magnets and motors in it. Now I've got this computer. DOES ANYONE REALLY UNDERSTAND HOW THESE THINGS WORK? They tell me it is binary code, all ones and zeroes. How someone can make pictures move on my computer screen using ones and zeroes is beyond me.

When I was a *lot* younger I had a friend who was a Xerox repairman. I used to be fascinated when I would watch him work on the innards of a copying machine. Have you ever looked inside one of those? I can't begin to imagine how someone would be able to *conceptualize* and *create* a machine so complex! It amazed me! Or consider television. How can someone *imagine* and then *create* a way to send colored moving pictures through the air, only to be able to reconstitute them on someone's TV screen? Man's mind is amazing!

Of course, we were created using a great template. *So God created man in His own image, in the image of God created He him; male and female created He them.* Wow! It's no wonder that we can create such complexities. Have you ever seen what God has created? Dumb question. What I mean is, have you ever stopped to really *look at* the things that God has made? Consider, if you will, the leaf. Just the simple and lowly leaf. It is a wonder of engineering, with veins to move nutrients and the ability to use sunlight for photosynthesis. Amazing!

Or how about the bumblebee? I love this one! According to MAN's laws of aerodynamics, for its body size and wing size, the bumblebee can't fly. Don't tell that to the bumblebee. Nor to its designer—God.

Look all around you. *The heavens declare the glory of God; and the firmament showeth His handiwork.* How can anyone see the magnificence around us and not believe in God? How can man, in his ignorance and hubris, think that all of this could have been created simply by chance?

Look at a sunrise (or a sunset, for us late risers). Marvel in the colors and the textures and the clouds. Admire and honor the artwork…and thank the artist. Thank HIM!

Blessings!

Sunday Musings
18

Beloved,

    I read Bill Bennett's *THE DEATH OF OUTRAGE*, last night. It triggered some thoughts I also had while reading one of Phillip Yancey's books. In the United States we have taken our freedom and turned it into license on an increasing basis.

    Follow me on this: 60 or 70 years ago we Americans were pretty strait-laced. Oh, sure, during the Roaring '20's we had the flappers and bathtub gin and such, but there was still an ethic practiced. There was still some restraint. We lived our lives as though there were some fundamental truths in the world. We believed in right and wrong. Gray was a color, not a variation of truth.

    As we got more cosmopolitan, or "European," as Bennett puts it, we starting looking at things differently. In the '60's we underwent a small revolution, where "free sex" and drugs and thumbing one's nose at authority became, if not the norm, acceptable. Situation ethics. If it feels good, do it. I'm not hurting anybody else, so leave me alone. "Turn on, tune in, drop out." The ACLU started telling us that we cannot abridge anyone's constitutional rights, and the Supreme Court began interpreting the Constitution to mean that virtually anything goes…as long as it is desired by small groups, minorities not the majority. This resulted in prayer being outlawed in school, the Ten Commandments being outlawed in public places, homosexuality being forced upon a heterosexual world as normal, adultery being accepted as approved because "everyone does it," and lying about sex being ok because "it's only about sex." Legalize marijuana, because everyone uses it (do you think he really didn't inhale?). We know what's best for *us*. It's like we, as a country, are immature (mentally retarded?) children. The chronologically older we become, the more "rights" we demand, even though it may be at the expense of others. "We're 'grown ups,' now. You can't tell *us* what to do." "We'll show you!"

Now we are so "grown up" that we have *outlawed* teachers disciplining students. As a result we have students physically attacking teachers. We are so "cosmopolitan" that we don't want to stifle our children by telling them what is right or wrong. As a result we have children who have no basis for their ethics or morals except what they see on television, and we have incidents like the student massacre at Columbine. We are so "European" that we practice *recreational* sex and adultery. As a result, we have a divorce rate, a failure of marriage commitments, over 50%. We have as entertainment, "games" which one Army general has likened to simulations that the military uses to teach soldiers how to kill and become inured to killing. We have given convicted criminals more rights and benefits in their jail cells than many free and non-criminal citizens have in the streets.

Isn't it great being grown up and allowed to make our own choices? Without any guidance? Determining for ourselves what is right and good and proper? We've done such a demonstrably good job of it.

Where did we go wrong? What can we do to get our acts straight? George Washington once said, "It is impossible to rightly govern the world without God and the Bible." Worked for George Washington. Upon the successful signing of the Declaration of Independence Samuel Adams said, "We have this day restored the Sovereign, to Whom alone men ought to be obedient. He reigns in heaven and…from the rising to the setting sun, may His Kingdom come." Ben Franklin said, "In the beginning of the contest with Britain, when we were sensible of danger, we had daily prayers in this room for Divine protection. Our prayers, Sir, were heard, and they were graciously answered. All of us who were engaged in the struggle must have observed frequent instances of a superintending Providence in our favor… And have we now forgotten this powerful Friend? Or do we imagine we no longer need His assistance?" Kind of sounds like where we are now doesn't it?

When I was a salesman we used to say, "silence indicates assent." In other words, if the customer doesn't say "No," then he is saying yes. So, if we allow these things to happen without raising our voices in complaint, if we turn our backs and pretend that it just doesn't matter, if we allow this smut to be forced into acceptance in our country without screaming bloody murder then we are assenting to it.

Is it too late? Have we allowed our moral and ethical decline to go too far? No. The answer is found in the book of Chronicles: ...*if My people, who are called by My name, shall humble themselves and pray, and seek My face and turn from their wicked ways, then will I hear from heaven, and will forgive their sin and will heal their land.* Maybe we should give it a try. Think about it.

Blessings!

Sunday Musings
19

Beloved,

Do you believe in dreams? No, that's not right. Do you believe that interpretation of your dreams will tell you "deep" things about yourself? Did you hear about the man who dreamed he was eating a giant marshmallow, and when he woke up he couldn't find his pillow? [Sorry.]

I had an interesting dream last night. In it I was teaching in a small seminar setting. Small groups of people would cycle through each of several sessions in this large hall, and in mine I was trying to teach them to sing. It was kind of fun. First I would teach them to get a beat, and then we would get into the music. A number of the participants were reticent. They did not want to participate because they felt they couldn't carry a tune. I tried to encourage them. Just for the joy of it. I would remind them that the Psalms say, "Make a joyful *noise* unto the Lord, all ye lands." (Ps 101:1) God isn't hung up on the beauty of the sound. It is the *intent* that counts with Him. It's what's inside, not what comes out.

Don't you wish *people* could be like this…could see the inner person and love the intent, if disappointed by the actual? Don't you wish that *you* could see past the aggravating superficial to be able to fully love the blessed "inner?" Sure it's easier to get "wrapped around the axle" by what we perceive. I teach my marketing and leadership classes that "perception is reality." So we need to fine-tune our perceptions to go beneath the exterior and distinguish the true value and intent. Tough to do? Yes, of course it is. Necessary? You tell me. Think about it.

Blessings!

Sunday Musings
20

Beloved,

Tolerance. That's a word we hear a lot of, nowadays. *Tolerance.* "…sympathy or indulgence for beliefs or practices differing from or conflicting with one's own." Sounds nice, doesn't it? Kind of makes you warm and fuzzy.

Tolerance. Shouldn't we all be more *tolerant*? For those of us who are Christians, followers of "The Way," isn't that something we should be practicing? With what is going on in the social and political world today, that's something that we are told we should be doing. If we are going to be "good people," then we should be tolerant—at least that's what we are told.

Those of us who are followers of "The Way" consider ourselves Christians. Isn't that what Jesus would have us do? Wasn't Jesus tolerant? *(Mt 21:12) And Jesus went into the temple of God and cast out all those who sold and bought in the temple, and overthrew the tables of the moneychangers, and the seats of those who sold doves.* Somehow, that doesn't sound…well, tolerant. Not to me.

What does it mean to be tolerant? Does it mean having to accept abortion even though you feel that it is murder? Does it mean to accept laws mandating homosexual preference, even though you believe that equality means *no one* should have preferential treatment? Does it mean accepting the unethical personal behavior of elected officials as long as it isn't affecting *our* pocketbooks? Tolerance. Doesn't tolerance mean accepting people and behavior that we truly believe is wrong? *(Mt 12:34) Offspring of vipers! How can you, being evil, speak good things?* That's what Jesus asked of the scribes and Pharisees. He, being good, would not tolerate that which was bad…which was evil…which He saw was wrong.

Tolerance. It is a squishy, warm and fuzzy buzzword which leads one to the situation ethics belief, so popular in the '60's and '70's—"if it feels good, do it." "Don't knock it if you haven't tried it." "It's *my* life, so you keep your nose out of it." There's no such thing as "absolute truth."

Well, there is, you know. There *are* absolute truths. There *are* basics, whose truths are immutable, and to have *tolerance* for those who knowingly and willingly violate and abrogate these **ABSOLUTE TRUTHS** is endorsing and affirming their transgression. *Tolerance,* the Christian way? Think about it.

Blessings

Sunday Musings
21

Beloved,

Last night, as we pulled in to the church, there was a car parked on the lawn with its hood up, and a young lady standing next to it. I didn't stop. I figured, considering where we were, she was OK. I didn't stop. I should have. She was a "plant." The pastor's lesson, this weekend, was on compassion, and the point that the pastor was making is that there are people all around us who can use our help…all we need do is *observe*. We don't have to *search for them.* Just keep our eyes open and *see*.

A year or so ago my best friend Harvey was driving up Flamingo Road and he passed a small pickup truck on the side of the road. A little further up the road was a man walking, obviously from the "dead" pickup. Harvey doesn't pick up hitchhikers and, in fact, the man wasn't hitching. But for some reason Harvey just felt that he should stop, and did. The man had run out of gas in his boss' pickup, was late getting back to work, and was worried. Harvey took him to his home, let him call his boss, got a gas can, took him to get gas, and took him back to his truck. During all of this, Harvey had a religious station on his radio, and chatted with the man about God. Didn't preach. Just let him know that Harvey's love for the Lord was why he felt directed to stop for the man. What kind of impression do you think that made?

Another friend of mine went to the gas station, the other day, and while he was pumping gas in his own car he observed an old lady pull up to the air hose and start trying to check the air in her tires. It was kind of difficult for her. She was elderly. Another man at the station, a scruffy looking guy, went over, took the tire gauge from her and checked and filled all of her tires. My friend went inside, and anonymously paid for the other man's tank of gas to show that his good deed had been observed and appreciated by others. Would you have *observed* that old lady? Would you have *done* anything?

Another friend of mine was driving down a North Carolina highway in the heat of a summer afternoon, and he saw a car broken down on the shoulder of the road with an elderly couple sitting in it. What would you have done? Would you figure that the Highway Patrol would be along shortly and they would be taken care of? After all, you don't know anything about auto mechanics. My friend thought about his own elderly parents, and knew that he would want someone to stop for them. He stopped, picked the couple up, drove them back about fifteen miles to their home so that they could get their other car and arrange for a tow. What did it cost him? A little time. What did it gain him? Perhaps another star on his crown in Heaven.

It says in the Bible that you should be kind to strangers because in so doing some have unknowingly entertained angels.

Then there was the friend of mine who was driving up the Florida Turnpike at 10:30 one night. On the shoulder was a broken down SUV, and a hundred yard up the road was a figure walking. What do you do? It's the middle of the night. "Black as Dick's hatband." No one else around. In crime-ridden south Florida. What do you do? He stopped, and the young man who had been driving home from class at the University, only needed to borrow a cell phone to call his mother to arrange for a tow. He would have had another five miles to walk, in the dark, before he found a pay phone. As he left, he called back to my friend, "God bless you!"

There's need all around us. There are simple things that all of us can do to assist others without putting ourselves out. Can we? *Do we? Do you?* Think about it.

Blessings!

Sunday Musings
22

Beloved,

I substituted in an interesting college class, yesterday. The course was TECHNOLOGY AND COMMUNICATIONS. Lots of discussion with the students, and it brought up some neat ideas. Think about it…communications in religion have gone from monks with quills to word processing, from parchment to bits and bytes and fiber optics. Amazing! Gave me some great sermon titles and topics: How about "The Ethical Seduction of Television?" "The Sacred Community in Secular Life." "Has Technology Outrun Ethics?"

I guess my drift is kind of obvious, huh? When you stop to think about it I'm afraid evil has a head start on good in using technology. (Don't believe in good and evil? Might as well stop reading now.)

How do I get away with making such a statement? The proof is all there. Do you know what the most active search topic is, in all search engines on the Internet? Sex. By a *huge* margin. That's not good, is it? And that's the Internet. How about video games? Do you think that all of the killing and violence is a good release for kids? That's what the producers of those games would have you believe. An Army General, however, has stated that they are the same kind of training that the Army gives to soldiers to prepare them for, and inure them to, death and destruction. That's not very good is it?

One thing that is very seducing to me is the television. Not that I am watching bad things [well, I have to admit I enjoy Mel Gibson movies], but I am talking about the *time* I waste watching TV instead of doing other things. I compare the time that I spend in front of the TV with the time I spend daily reading the Bible…or just reading *anything*, and it is embarrassing. It's certainly not a **good** use of my limited time.

We had a discussion, too, about putting smut filters on public-access computers to keep kids from getting to X-rated websites. To get the discussion going I complained that this censorship would be a violation of the First Amendment to the Constitution. It seems that the class pretty much agreed that some degree of censorship, in the interest of *common decency*, was not only acceptable but also preferable. I guess it's the question of where does freedom end and license begin. We certainly support the Constitution, but it's there to protect our way of life, isn't it? Is letting our way of life become deeply stained by pornography good? Which is the greater evil?

Then there is the fact that e-technology enables anonymity, and allows a lapse of moral bases. Do you really think as many people would be spending as much time in pornography if their identities were known? Did you hear about the Divinity School Dean who had a college-owned computer at home? When it acted up he had a tech from the college come out to fix it. When the tech found numerous pornographic websites accessed from the computer the Dean, in disgrace, had to resign. Would he have spent as much time in pursuing smut if he hadn't thought he had this technological anonymity?

No, I'm not saying we need to go back to pre-technological times. It is my belief, though, that we need to realize the challenge that exists for those of us who believe in the existence of good and evil and absolute truths. How about you? Think about it.

Blessings!

Sunday Musings
23

Beloved,

You know the song, "My Favorite Things?" *Raindrops on roses, and whiskers on kittens...* There is a similar one in many hymnals: *Count your many blessings, name them one-by-one...* Have you ever stopped to think about *your* favorite things?

I've got clinical depression. Oh, it's not that big a deal, now. It's under control. But when it was raging, I didn't see many "favorite things." It was a real struggle to count *any*, much less *many*, blessings. You say you've "been there, done that?" You may not be in depression, but you can still be depressed. Or you can be so *oppressed* that you don't much feel like you are blessed.

Today, it seems that "favorite things" most often are possessions. What is your favorite thing? Your *Ski Nautique*? Your BMW? Your summer home in the mountains of North Carolina? Or are your favorite things the ones for which you are still striving? That million-dollar portfolio, or membership at the country club, or skybox at the stadium? Maybe that's why we are overwhelmed, rather than satisfied. Maybe that's why we feel that "the *hurrier* we go the *behinder* we get."

Every day, it seems, someone is asking where the time has gone. We are so over-scheduled, so over-committed, so overwhelmed with the demands of living today that nothing seems to get through our reactive armor. As soon as some external stimulus comes into contact with us, we immediately explode back at it, and keep it from penetrating. We don't have time for that. Got to keep moving. They can't hit a moving target. Go, go, go, go!

Well, STOP! No, this isn't another "stop and smell the roses." Are you feeling overwhelmed, discouraged, depressed? Stop, sit down, and *write a list* of your favorite things. Your blessings. Sitting with the cat on your lap, purring as you stroke her ears. The way the Trumpet

Plant's blossoms smell in the night. The way the sun sets so beautifully over the lake. The raucous way the parrots squawk as they fly by in a green cloud. The beauty of the Great Blue Heron standing stately still by the canal…waiting for dinner. Or for those of you up north, the way the wind whispers in the dark trees on a snowy evening. The perkiness of the first robin of spring. The way the first purple crocuses poke up through the snow. Make the list. Read it. Savor it. And the next time it happens, the next time you get "down in the dumps," make a new list. *Count your blessings, name them one by one.*

Blessings!

Sunday Musings
24

Beloved,

I want to share a couple of things with you:

After my New Year's letter, dealing with lack of service in stores, my sister wrote and told me this about where she lives (in Swarthmore, PA):

> People in shops are usually very friendly and helpful. I should add that the people who live in this area are not at all friendly in a public way. They don't even look at you in stores etc., let along speak to you. But the help is great. Our grocery store has a few retarded employees and a bunch of retirees…particularly men who bag groceries and bring in the baskets from the lot. They look like they retired from middle management jobs and their wives wanted them out of the house. Several are tremendously extroverted and once one even sang to me as he bagged my groceries. They are always up and cheerful and that is reflected in the feeling in the store. The extreme extrovert, Mario, sometimes leads choruses of happy birthday over the loud speaker and dresses up like Santa Claus and cavorts around the store. There are a bunch of thank you letters up on the wall to Mario from classes he has toured around the store. And, yes, I think we all need to do our bit to improve the situation. On our way home from 11 pm church Christmas Eve, we stopped to buy Cascade in the all night CVS. I added a chocolate Santa to my order and then gave it to the checkout girl. And that was before you wrote your sermon.

That is reassuring. Suburban Philadelphia is not where I would expect to find this. Rural areas, yes. North Carolina, yes. But not in such a northern urban area.

Here's something else I'd like to share. It was sent to me quite some time ago by one of my daughter's grad school profs:

Back when the telegraph was the fastest means of long-distance communication, a young man applied for a job as a Morse code operator. When he arrived for the interview, he entered a large, noisy office. In the background a telegraph clacked away. A sign on the wall instructed job applicants to fill out a form and wait until they were summoned to enter the inner office. The young man completed his form and sat down with seven other waiting applicants. After a few minutes, the young man stood up, crossed the room to the door of the inner office, and walked right in. Within a few minutes the young man emerged from the inner office escorted by the interviewer, who announced to the other applicants, "Gentlemen, thank you very much for coming, but the job has been filled by this young man." The other applicants began grumbling to each other, and then one spoke up saying, "Wait a minute, I don't understand something. He was the last one to come in, and we never even got a chance to be interviewed. Yet he got the job. That's not fair!" The employer responded, "I'm sorry, but all the time you've been sitting here, the telegraph has been ticking out the following message in Morse code: 'If you understand this message, then come right in. The job is yours.' None of you heard it or understood it. This young man did. So the job is his."

We live in a noisy world, yet God still speaks to us through His word and His Spirit. Are you listening?

We are now in a new year, and truly a new millennium. Let's pray that we can see a different spirit in our country. Not necessarily the *bipartisanship* the media and politicians are talking about. The spirit that we need is not new. What we need is a rebirth of the ethics, the mores, and the spiritual values on which this country of ours was founded.

Blessings!

Sunday Musings
25

Beloved,

Tom Smith is our landlord at Smith's Beach in Virginia. Tom, a bachelor, and his brother used to live together in the big farmhouse up the road behind the Beach. One day Tom and his brother got into a big argument. Fuming with anger his brother went out to the grassy field behind the house, climbed into his little airplane, and took off. Tom, intending to have the last laugh (if not the last word) went to the barn, cranked up the tractor, and plowed the landing field. Anger drove them apart, and angry actions kept them apart.

Anger is an ordinary natural emotion. To get angry is not abnormal or necessarily wrong. What is wrong is to let our anger get the better of us. What is wrong is to lose our temper and do something unwise. What is wrong is to allow anger and resentment to fester, to burn, to rot. What is wrong is to get angry and hold a grudge. That's when our anger becomes destructive.

I'm often asked by students or friends how to deal with the anger they have for someone. They feel that they have been hurt so badly, wronged so severely, cut so deeply that they cannot manage to forgive. They are hurting and resenting and mourning. They feel damaged, forsaken, persecuted. But you know something? More often than not, the person with whom they are upset doesn't realize it. *They* are not angry or hurt. They are going on with their lives; apparently oblivious to the devastation they have left behind. My question to those who are hurting, who are nurturing their pain is this: who's winning? Not that it's a contest, but who is still distressed? Who is losing sleep? Whose life is still upset? If you are the one who is unhappy, and the other person doesn't even know about it…LET IT GO! For Pete's sake! What good is it doing *you* to maintain the pain? LET IT GO!

OK, so what if there is a mutuality of hurt? The other member is angry. They, too, are still wounded and hurting. What then? The answer then is pretty well documented. WORK IT OUT *NOW!* Don't wait. Don't keep putting it off. WORK IT OUT *NOW!* Marriage counselors tell us never to go to bed angry at our partner…stay up and talk until spousal problems are worked out. In the Bible we are told not to let the sun set on our anger. It's good advice. Don't let the mutually held anger grow and worsen. It won't take too long before a virtually unbridgeable chasm will form. WORK IT OUT *NOW!*

Finally, don't do as Tom Smith did. It's a funny story, but don't put up obstacles to reconciliation. Don't let your anger and hurt keep the other party away. Don't force the pain to persist. Don't insist that the estrangement continue.

Let's face it, folks: life is too short and relationships too valuable to allow them to languish and die. Get angry, if you must, but get over it, *you must!*

Is there anyone you are mad at, now, and they don't know it? Is there anyone with whom you share a hurt and anger? In the Bible we are told when we bring our sacrifice to the Temple to search ourselves and see if we have strife with anyone, and if so, to go and correct it before worshipping. Do you hold ought against your brother? Why? Think about it.

Blessings!

Sunday Musings
26

Beloved,

♫ *"Raindrops on roses, and whiskers on kittens…"* ♫

I was reading a book by Marlin Maddox, this week, which triggered a memory. Over ten years ago I was in the hospital for ten weeks. For the first two weeks I was in a Neurological Intensive Care Unit (NICU), paralyzed from the neck down. I can't complain about the care I received. It was wonderful. And Chris got down to visit me every day. And I had television. And music. And mail. But you know what one of the most wonderful things was? Twice each day they wheeled me from the NICU, down through the ER, out the back door, and into the trailer housing the decompression chamber. I'd spend from three to seven hours in the chamber before being wheeled back to my NICU room. The wonderful part? Between the ER door and the trailer I got to breathe salt air, see Biscayne Bay, and feel the sun on my face. It was so wonderful! Every once in a while the guys would leave me lying in the sun for a few minutes before taking me back into the hospital. Man, that felt good! Now and then it would be raining when they wheeled me in or out. Then I'd get to feel the wet breeze, and get an occasional sprinkle of rain on my face. That, too, was very special.

♫ *"Count your many blessings, name them one-by-one…"* ♫

Unfortunately, when we stop to count our blessings, if we don't have **big** ones to note, we don't think we have any [or many] blessings. How shortsighted! There are some old guys at the gym where I work out who have the right idea. They recognize that waking up each morning is a blessing. How about sunrises and sunsets? Isn't the ability to see them a blessing? How about the laughter of children? Can you hear it? Isn't that a blessing? Those of you up north have seen the crocuses poking up through the snow, the forsythia starting to bloom, and the first robins coming back. Isn't the ability to see and appreciate them a blessing? Have you ever listened to Mozart's *Eine Kleine Nachtmusik?* What a blessing! What makes you think that the only blessings worth counting are winning the lottery or marrying the beauty queen?

You know, it's completely up to you. It is your choice whether you are going to let that S.O.B. that cut you off in traffic ruin your day, or if you are going to ignore him and, rather, see that hawk soaring on a thermal up over that field. It is your choice whether you are going to curse the pollen that is causing you to sneeze, or wipe your nose and appreciate the beautiful flowers. It is your choice whether you want to curse the darkness, or look up and see the stars and the moon. Happiness is a choice. Satisfaction is a choice. Love is a choice. I love life and I love everything that the Lord has given me. How about you? Think about it

Blessings!

Sunday Musings
27

Beloved,

Have you read *TUESDAYS WITH MORRIE*, yet? DO IT!! It's a great book. I was rereading it this past week, and I noted one spot where Mitch, the author, wrote about how Morrie craved the *touch* of friends. Human touch. It is a reassurance of your being. It is a statement of acceptance, friendship, and love. Of comfort and consolation. I had a chiropractor, once, whose touch felt…well, good. No, I'm not saying that she had a "healing" touch. I'm not sure how or what, but she just had a good touch.

In the book *THE FIVE LOVE LANGUAGES* [another book I *strongly* recommend], one of the languages is touch. That is how some people want to be communicated with. Touch. I know it is one of my *languages*. Not necessarily anything suggestive. I love it when I am driving and Chris just simply reaches over and rubs the back of my neck. Just the touch of a friend or loved one. It's reassuring. Soothing. Comforting.

Now, I admit that some people do not want to be touched. They cringe from it. They covet their privacy. And in the Leading and Managing course I am teaching, right now, it notes how it is virtually impossible for someone to touch someone who is senior to them in the pecking order. You have to know the person with whom you are dealing. It is kind of the way Zig Ziglar put it. You've heard of the Golden Rule? Zig talks about the Platinum Rule. That's "Do unto others the way they *want* to be done unto." In other words, figure out what people want, and give it to them. And a lot of people want, crave, touch.

Reading *TUESDAYS WITH MORRIE* reminded me of when my father was dying and I was sitting with him. I gently rubbed his forearm, as he was lying in his hospital bed, and he said how good it felt.

The human touch. Of course, it made me feel bad that I hadn't realized this need of Dad's before.

Anyway, that's my message for this week. As the phone company used to say, "Reach out and touch someone." Read those who mean something to you, and if touch is in their personal lexicon, then touch them. I didn't realize until about 10 hours before Dad died that he wanted it. Don't wait that long with the ones you love.

Blessings!

Sunday Musings
28

Beloved,

I was at a family reunion in Philadelphia over the weekend. It was wonderful seeing the cousins, and the second cousins (the cousins' kids), and the third cousins (the cousins' kids' kids). And over all were the three Aunts…the matriarchs of the clan. It was fun.

But as I was flying home, reflecting on the reunion, it struck me that even these people, many of whom had known me since I was "little Davy," don't look at me as the boiled down essential "me." Even to them my being is tainted by what I've done, or titles I've acquired. Lieutenant Commander (ret.). The Reverend. Professor. Bud and Dot's son. Judy's brother. All true, but at all relevant?

Another book for your Must Read List: *In The Name of Jesus* by Henri Nouwen. In this little book Nouwen reflects upon his trip from Harvard professor to worker at the Daybreak community for mentally handicapped people. The residents didn't care what degrees he had earned or been awarded, what he had achieved in his years of study and teaching.

> *I was suddenly faced with my naked self, open for affirmations and rejections, hugs and punches, smiles and tears, all dependent simply on how I was perceived at the moment. …Reputations could no longer be counted on…it forced me to rediscover my true identity…that unadorned self.*

Wow! What a fascinating—and frightening—concept.

Stop and try to wrap your mind around that. Think of who we *really are.* Jackie and Carol, try to ignore that your students see you as TEACHER. Janie, discount that you are COMMANDER and Bob, that you are CAPTAIN. Brooke and Brad, Dan and Herb, do not take into account that you are PASTOR. Forget relationships, connections, accomplishments and reputations. Who are **we *really*?**

You know, God doesn't care about all of this superficial fluff. I've often quoted the bumper sticker—**GOD LOVES YOU WHETHER YOU WANT HIM TO OR NOT.** Nouwen says, *God loves us not because of what we do or accomplish, but because God has created and redeemed us in love...* I guess it's a variation of the Protestant "you are redeemed by faith and not works."

I hope that I have given us all something to think about. Strip away all of the superfluous and who are we really? Are our goals and priorities what they *should* be? When we artichoke-like peel away all of the top layers and get down to the heart, do we really like what we find? If we consider that being relevant, popular and powerful are not vocations but temptations are we satisfied with who we have become?

> *The desire to be relevant and successful will gradually disappear, and our only desire will be to say with our whole being to our brothers and sisters of the human race, "You are loved. There is no reason to be afraid. In love God created your inmost self and knit you together in your mother's womb"(see Psalm 139:13).* (Nouwen)

In America of today it's kind of radical to think of ourselves as separate from our accomplishments, but try it just for me. Try it for yourself. Try it because when we come "before the Throne," He won't care what we've accomplished temporally. He'll only look for His love in us. Whether it is there and shining forth to others. Will it be there in you? Will others be able to see it? Will HE? Think about it.

Blessings!

Sunday Musings
29

Beloved,

I officiated at a wedding, yesterday. You know, not having my own pastorate means that when I am honored to do a wedding it is a very personal blessing for me. I just love it when a friend asks me to be their minister for such a special and sacred time. Anyway, yesterday was typical of so many weddings. To begin with, the coordinator at the country club made a scheduling mistake, so we had to change from an evening wedding to a morning wedding. When, just before the ceremony, the men put on their tuxedos they found that some had cummerbunds, some had vests, and there were several different varieties of ties. [Yes, they all came from the same rental place. Who checks the *tuxes* beforehand, for pity sake?] The couple had obtained the wedding license some weeks ago, and put it in a safe place. Unfortunately they couldn't remember where that safe place was. They wanted to do a Unity Candle, but no one was quite sure of how to get the mothers' candles lit. When we finally got started, we were about 30 minutes late.

But, you know what? IT ALL WORKED OUT FINE AND NOBODY CARED ABOUT THE LITTLE STUFF! The bride was beautiful, the groom handsome, the flower girl adorable. The roses were magnificent, and the pastor...oh, he was just superb!

The point being, this was all being done according to God's laws, in God's time, and God's way. How could it possibly not go well? It's a lesson that we all should learn. I have a colorful window-hanger that says, ***LET GO & LET GOD***. I know that the secular humanists will consider this a cop-out, but being able to turn our worries over to The Lord, who never rests and is always ready and anxious to take on our problems, is a relief.

So, let me urge you—if you don't know God, you should get acquainted. And if you already are in a relationship with Him, believe it when He says: *Come unto me all ye who labour and are heavy laden, and I will give you rest.*

Blessings!

Sunday Musings
30

Beloved,

There's a fascinating column by the Editor of NEW MOBILITY magazine, this month. In it Barry Corbet points out "we [the disabled] work hard to convince nondisabled people that our lives are just fine...we keep our sorrows close to the vest." He then notes that "disability shreds all our presumptions of freedom, authenticity or confidence...most of us [once we become disabled] must find our adventures elsewhere." The column is entitled "The Conquest of the Ordinary," and its gist is that "people with disabilities...are engaged in the conquest of the ordinary. We find adventure in reaching the unreachable object, in scratching the unscratchable itch." "A parallel trick of living with a disability...is to see all and everything as an adventure, one that endows every moment with all the most adventuresome qualities—uncertainty and risk, richness and joy, deliberation and derring-do"—an intriguing insight. Corbet used to enjoy overseas treks into rugged and untamed areas, a pastime now proscribed by his physical limitations. Philosophically he recognizes that he, like other disabled, is living a *new reality* in which we must recognize that what yesterday was the simple and commonplace, today is the challenging, defiant and exciting.

But let's take this beyond just those of us who are disabled. All of us, the physically whole as well as the physically broken, should consider the implications of this approach to life. Who among us, as we grow physically older, or gain more familial responsibility, or become more invaluable to our employers, or just plain "chicken out," do not feel a loss...an inability to escape from our humdrum everyday lives?

The real problem, as I see it, is how we see our "humdrum everyday lives." They are only tedious and unexciting if we allow them to be. No, I'm not talking about the thrill of staying alive on a daily commute down I-95 into Miami (or Washington or Philadelphia or NYC). Don't you realize how exciting it is just to live and love every day?

Oh, my life is so boring.

Well, consider the alternative. Somehow, not waking up seems somewhat more tedious to me.

Yeah, but everyday it's the same old thing.

OK. Do you have kids or grandchildren? Are they *in stasis,* or does every day see something new in their lives?

Well, no, the kids are gone so I don't see them much.

You're going to be a hard case, aren't you? Let me tell you about my mother. She's gone, now, but above my computer I have a picture of Mom peering into a kaleidoscope. I guess she was about 82 when it was taken. You can tell by the look on her face that she is really enjoying seeing the swirling forms and colors. Now, do you think she had never seen a kaleidoscope until then? No indeed. But it could still evoke a sense of wonder in her. Even though she knew how it worked, it fascinated her. In fact, *everything* fascinated Mom. She couldn't just *look* at anything. She had to *examine* it…to see what it was made of…to see how it worked. Mom never saw a leaf that she didn't see a fascinating God-created factory that took water and sunlight and created food that it sent through a delicate network of veins and capillaries throughout the plant. Mom never saw just a seashell, but always saw how the calcium forming the shell was layered, as the mollusk grew bigger, and how the muscle of the bivalve was attached and worked.

Mom was that way with people, too. Mom never got a ride from a taxi driver…it was always a *person* who had parents and a family and a life outside their hack. It was the same with everyone with whom she dealt. Even if she didn't actually talk with them (though most of the time she did), she wondered about their lives.

Everything fascinated Mom. Once, when she had heart failure in the hospital, they had to intubate her…put a tube down her throat into her lungs to drain fluid and mechanically breathe for her. When she recovered she just *had* to see the tube, to see how big it was, to measure how far down into her it had gone, to see how it was made and how it worked. If it happened in life, Mom wanted to know about it.

When Mother finally died, if there was a flicker of consciousness, I'll bet she was excited and fascinated by this new adventure upon which she was embarking. That's the way that she was. Life challenged and excited and fascinated her. There was no such thing as the common-place—just exciting things that she had done or seen once before.

So, what's your excuse? I'm crippled, but only physically. I still am challenged by the conquest of the ordinary every day. The good Lord has given me the ability to think and feel and react and enjoy...to sense and experience and observe and reflect. How dare I, or how dare you, not make the most of what we have been so graciously given? Think about it.

Blessings!

Book Two

Sunday Musings
1

Beloved,

My datebook has pithy "thoughts" at the top of each page to stimulate thought. Well, it worked. This one, today, was a quote from Hugh Walpole:

> *The whole secret to life is to be interested in one thing profoundly and in a thousand other things well.*

It rather reminded me of my mother. Mom never met anything that didn't deeply interest her. I have, in my desk drawer, a 10X magnifier that she used to carry with her, just so that she could get a good look at...well, anything. Have you ever looked at something under 10X magnification? What? Well, try your hand, for instance. Look closely at the ridges and whorls of your fingerprint. For that matter, look closely at the ridges and whorls of the palm of your hand. Kind of neat! I've got a chunk of coral on my desk. It's interesting to look at and to feel. But under magnification it's just...breathtaking.

I envy Mom her fascination with life. I have a picture of her on my desk peering through a kaleidoscope. She loved them, the way that they would refract and reflect light, and make commonplace things artistically beautiful. Everything that God has given us in this world is beautiful. You just have to know how to look at it.

I guess part of it is taking the commonplace and seeing that it really is miraculous. Like the song in the musical, **FLOWER DRUM SONG**. It goes something like this:

> *A hundred million miracles are happening every day,*
> *And those who say they don't agree*
> *Are those who do not hear or see.*

A swallow in Tasmania is sitting on her eggs,
And suddenly those eggs have wings and eyes and beaks and legs!
A hundred million miracles.

A little girl in Chunking, just thirty inches tall
Decides that she is going to walk and did it doesn't fall!
A hundred million miracles.

The miracles of God's world are all around us. We don't need the 10X magnifier to see them. Just look at a tree. Or the blossom on your hibiscus. Or the puffy white cumulus cloud. Think of how He made birds with hollow bones to help them fly, or how he makes the bumble bee fly in spite of the laws of aeronautics that say it is impossible.

A hundred million miracles. And all that you have to do is look at the world with eyes that see…and appreciate. Think about it. Pray about it. And praise God for the miracle of your own life.

Blessings!

Sunday Musings
2

Beloved,

Just close your eyes and picture this. NO! Wait a minute. If you close your eyes you won't be able to read the description. OK. Read it, then close your eyes and picture it.

Unless you have lived all your life in downtown Manhattan at some point you have seen the setting sun when it is just about on the horizon. You know…huge, brilliant orangey-red, incandescently glowing. Well, imagine that sun perfectly eclipsed by a large dark leafy tree. The fiery sun blazes through the tiny spaces around the black backlit leaves, glinting dazzlingly, making the tree seem on fire but unconsumed. The orb is so large that around the edge of the tree is a luminous rosy aura, a shimmering corona. You have to look quickly. The sun is sinking, and tomorrow night the earth's season travel will have moved it just far enough to misalign the components. But if you catch it, if you are in the right place at the right time, the unimaginable glory of God's artwork is breathtaking.

I just had to share it with you. God shared it with me.

Blessings!

Sunday Musings
3

Beloved,

As I sit writing the London Philharmonic Orchestra and Philharmonic Choir are performing Handel's *The Messiah* on my CD player. WOW!

So, tomorrow is Christmas. Christ's birthday. Tonight, at the Calvary Chapel Ft. Lauderdale Christmas Eve celebration 22,000 celebrants will lift lighted candles and sing "Happy birthday to you; happy birthday to you; happy birthday dear Jesus; happy birthday to you." A 2001st birthday celebration. Of course, Jesus wasn't born 2001 years ago, you know. I think it was a priest or monk named Dionysus who counted the number of years from Christ's birth until his own time to establish the official *Anno Domini* year. But he miscounted! When they went back and checked his arithmetic, it turns out that Dionysus had dropped a couple of years. Now Jesus wasn't born in year 0, He was born in 4 or 5 B.C.!

And Jesus wasn't born on December 25th, either. It was Julius I, Bishop of Rome, who chose that date in 350 A.D. (which, as you and I know, was actually 354 or 355 AD, but who's counting?) After worshiping Him for three and one-half centuries they decided it would be nice to have a D.O.B., so Julius went for the 25th. You see, he wanted a date that would clash with the winter solstice, which was a pretty big thing pagan-wise. Julius wanted to take a little of the seasonal wind out of their sails.

And the gifts and lights and decorated tree? Well, they come from the Roman celebration of Saturnalia…worship of the pagan god Saturn. They had a month-long party, with garlands of laurel decorating their homes and candles burning on the trees and gifts for everyone. Saturn was a cool guy. Party Down! (And did you know that Emperor Constantine insisted that the Sabbath be moved from Saturday to Sunday…because he still had kind of a soft spot for worshiping the sun god?)

So, let's see. Jesus wasn't born 2001 years ago. And it wasn't on December 25th. And the decorations and gifts and merriment are from a pagan celebration. But, you know what? IT JUST DON'T MAT-TER! 'Cause no matter the date, Jesus WAS born. And no matter why the parties started, they carry on now in celebration of HIS birthday. WHENEVER IT WAS. Want to pick nits? Go do it somewhere else. Jesus is real. Jesus was born. Jesus did live, and is still alive. We are celebrating his birth NOW. All the rest is just static…an opportunity for those whose lives are empty of the Saviour to complain. Don't let their whining bother you. Just nod knowingly, smile sympathetically, and then join with the angels singing,

> **Joy to the world,**
> **The Lord has come,**
> **Let earth receive her King.**

And although it is politically incorrect, let me wish you a very merry Christmas, and a very blessed 2002. (Or is it 2007?)

Blessings!

Sunday Musings
4

Happy New Year!!!!

Gee! Another year gone, and now an opportunity for another new beginning. Are you getting geared up? Have you made your New Year's Resolutions, yet? Are you going to lose that extra weight *this New Year*? Or are you going to quit smoking *this New Year*? Those are the two primary ones. Tomorrow is a New Year. An opportunity for us to change things. Change our lives. Change our futures. All that we need to do is to make some New Year's Resolutions and let the New Year carry us along into success. Right.

New Year's Resolutions. For me they have always been an exercise in futility. Yet, once again, I am going to use this subjective point in the continuum of time as a base to try to springboard myself into some sort of change. I guess that is one of the endearing things about human nature. No matter how many times we have been shown that New Year's resolutions don't work, we are still hopeful enough to try again. We are always hopeful of changing ourselves…to create a better "me."

So, what's your hope for the New Year? To lose weight? To make your first million? To be a better…father, salesman, husband, manager, tennis player, golfer? Or maybe yours is even a deeper hope and need. Maybe you are resolving, in the New Year, to become a better *person*. In my case, of course, that means a better Christian. *I resolve in the year 2002 to try to mold my life to be more like Jesus Christ.* Whew! That one is a biggie. Of course it is something that all followers of *The Way* strive for every day. Actually, it is the only way to guarantee that you will be able to change your life…to create a better "me." To be born again of The Spirit.

So, what's for you in the New Year? Are you making resolutions? If so, pray while you are making them. Pray that the resolutions you make will be directed not at making your life in 2002 successful. Pray that your life in 2002 will be *significant*.

Blessings!

Sunday Musings
5

Beloved,

According to the National Center for Health Statistics, 43% of all first marriages break up within 15 years. (NCHS Press Office, 5/24/ 01) FORTY-THREE PERCENT! That's terrible!

Another source has related that over 80% of married soldiers who returned from Viet Nam disabled in some fashion had their wives leave them. EIGHTY PERCENT!

As an ordained minister, it is my privilege and pleasure to perform the occasional wedding ceremony. The vows which I use state,

> *I take thee to be my wedded wife; to have and to hold from this day forward; for better for worse, for richer for poorer, in sickness and in health; to love and to cherish, until death separates us, according to God's holy laws: and to this I pledge you my faith.*

Those are the vows that most pledge to in a church wedding. ...*For better for worse, for richer for poorer, in sickness and in health.* We so easily make the pledge during the ceremony, in the flush of our new love, why is it so easy to forget it later on? Is it perhaps because we have become a disposable society? We've seemingly come to the point that if we don't like something, we are quick to dispose of it in order to try something different. We don't want to have to work at making it successful. We don't like to have to struggle. Not if we've got an easy way out. One source said, "Two recent studies independently concluded that the effects of the new divorce laws (no-fault) have increased the divorce rate in some jurisdictions 20 to 25 percent." In Florida, as recently as a few years ago, you could purchase a do-it-yourself divorce kit at the county courthouse for only $4.95. How cheaply some hold their marriage vows!

My parents would have been married 57 years the year that they died. Was it all easy for them and that's how they lasted so long? Did they not have to work at it? Be serious! When they married the Great Depression still had the country in its clutches. It ended when WWII began, and Dad went off to the war in the Pacific. I don't know all of their trials, but I do remember when Mom broke her back, and was laid up for months. Dad had to nurse her at home, while being both father and mother to my sister and me. They *worked* at their marriage. When problems came along, they met them, and defeated them.

Chris and I have been married for 34 years this past Friday. How have we lasted so long? Is it because we've had it so easy? Sure. Easy. Of course, our second anniversary was spent with me in Viet Nam. We've done without a lot of things while we were both college students, and while Chris stayed home with the kids instead of getting a job. And, of course, things were such a breeze when I spent ten weeks in the hospital (during which Hurricane Andrew blew right over top of us) only to emerge as a paraplegic.

A successful marriage takes a lot of things. Communication, trust, love…but perhaps most important it takes a trust in God and a lot of work—hard work—on both partner's parts. It is up to both of you to make your marriage work. Remember, the admonition at the end of the service applies not only to outsiders but also to the bride and groom—

**What therefore God hath joined together,
let not man put asunder.**

Happy Father's Day to you all.

Blessings!

Sunday Musings
6

Beloved,

Well, first thing—I was wrong. It's only been 33 years, not 34. Just seems like 34. Actually, since we started dating the month I turned 17, Chris and I have been together for 37 years, now.

Second, I had some responses to last week's *Musings* that prompted some more thought. Kind of sad responses. They reminded me about something else which I like to tell those whose marriage ceremonies I perform. A lot of people talk about marriage being a fifty-fifty proposition. Well, I'd like to state that is wrong. Marriage is not a fifty-fifty proposition. Marriage is a 100%-100% proposition. You cannot be only one-half dedicated to such an important relationship.

Unfortunately, as some of my correspondents reminded me, if one member is 100% dedicated but the other is not, then there is often a breakdown in the system...a failure of the marriage. Unfortunately, the one who *was* dedicated is the one that feels as though they are the failure. This makes it a double tragedy. I wish that I had a magic phrase that would alleviate the psychic pain. I don't. Boy, I wish I did. But this next segment should help.

◆   ◆   ◆

On a totally different note—I got a new Buck knife, a couple of weeks ago. You guys will understand. Buck knives, ladies, are one of the finest tools made. I've loved them since I was a Boy Scout. Anyway, there was a little brochure enclosed with the knife that I'd like to tell you about. It was from Chuck Buck, the present Chairman/CEO. Here's what it said:

> If this is your first Buck Knife, "welcome aboard." You are part of a very large family. Although we're talking about a few million peo-

ple, we still like to think of each one of our users as a member of the Buck Knives Family and take a personal interest in the knife that was bought. With normal use you should never have to buy another. *(Up to now, a pretty standard product message. Right?)*

Now that you are family, you might want to know a little more about our organization. The fantastic growth of Buck Knives, Inc. was no accident. From the beginning, management determined to make God the Senior partner. In a crisis, the problem was turned over to Him, and He hasn't failed to help us with the answer. Each knife must reflect the integrity of management, including our Senior Partner. If sometimes we fail on our end, because we are human, we find it imperative to do our utmost to make it right. Of course, to us, besides being Senior Partner, he is our heavenly Father also, and it's a great blessing to us to have this security in these troubled times. If any of you are troubled or perplexed and looking for answers, may we invite you to look to Him, for God loves you. *"For God loved the world so much that He gave His only son; so that anyone who believes in Him shall not perish but have eternal life."—John 3:16*

Kind of funny how that just happened to pop up at this time, isn't it? [Coincidence is God's way of letting you know that He's still there.] You see, that's the answer to the problem at the beginning of this letter. "Why did my marriage fail when I worked so hard at making it work?" As Mr. Buck put it, "If any of you are troubled or perplexed and looking for answers, may we invite you to look to Him, for God loves you." He does, you know. And He has promised not to put more upon you than you are able to handle—able to handle…with Him. Think about it. Pray about it. And remember:

God loves you, whether you want Him to or not.

Blessings!

Sunday Musings
7

Beloved,

The Golden Rule. QUICK! RECITE IT! Get it right? Of course you did. You've heard The Golden Rule since you were a child. And you don't have to be a Christian to know The Golden Rule. It exists, in one form or another, in most major world religions and philosophies. Just look:

> *Leviticus 19:18*—"you shall love your neighbor as yourself"

> *Matthew 22:39*—"Thou shalt love thy neighbour as thyself."

> *Confucius*—"Do unto another what you would have him do unto you, and do not do unto another what you would not have him do unto you. Thou needest this law alone. It is the foundation of all the rest."

> *Isocrates*—"Act toward others as you desire them to act toward you."

You know The Golden Rule. Do you practice it?

Let me tell you about Jimmy: A month before I ended up paralyzed we closed on a three-story house in Maryland. It took us a year before we could move up there (for me to go to graduate school), and we rented the house out in the meantime. There were, of course, times when it sat empty and we were a bit concerned about who was watching over it. Didn't need to be. Living next door to that house was Jimmy, a man to whom Jesus had said, *Thou shalt love thy neighbour as thyself.* Jimmy heard and obeyed. Jimmy didn't know Chris and me—had never met us. He only knew, from the realtor, that I had been incapacitated, and wouldn't be up for a while. So Jimmy took it upon himself to look over my house in Maryland. When it was empty he made sure that it was secure. He mowed the lawn. He raked the leaves. He shoveled the snow. I wasn't even his neighbor, yet, but Jimmy saw a need, and there was never any question in his mind—he took care of it.

After we got moved in to our Maryland house, Jimmy didn't stop. I could mow the lawn, walking rather awkwardly behind the mower and sometimes tumbling on the hill out back, and I wasn't used to people *doing* for me. I liked doing things for others. But Jimmy wouldn't stop. He wouldn't take anything for it; he just kept mowing the lawn. And raking. And shoveling. When we finished unpacking, and had put the cartons in the garage and driveway, Jimmy broke them up, put them in the back of his pickup truck, and drove them about 15 miles to the dump. I didn't ask. He just knew it needed doing, so he did it.

One day the doorbell rang, and there was Jimmy. We wanted me to move my car out of the driveway. He was going to pull his pickup truck in, put my stepladder in the back, and go up on MY roof to clean my gutters! Jimmy didn't want anything for all of this attention.

Even our thanks seemed to make him very uncomfortable. Jimmy was just doing what Jesus had told him to do. Oh, sure, I am sure that Jimmy's wife Jackie can tell us lots of things that are less-than-Christian about my beloved brother Jimmy. He is only human. But, I like to think that I am an aspiring Christian—someone like Jimmy, with his selfless and simple faith and action, puts me to shame.

How about you? "Oh," you say, "am I supposed to be my brother's keeper?" Watch it! That's what Cain asked (Genesis 4:9). I'm not going to answer it for you. You need to answer that question for yourself. Look around you. Look at the people you know. Heck, be like Jimmy and look at people you don't necessarily know, but you know of. Is there need around you that YOU can help? Can you? Should you? Think about it. Pray about it.

And, Jimmy—thank you and God bless you always. I do love you and miss you.

Blessings!

Sunday Musings
8

Beloved,

How strong are your beliefs? Do you have core values that guide your everyday life? How much do you really believe in them? Would you fight for them?

This is something I found while I was in the Coast Guard:

> War is an ugly thing. But not the ugliest of things: The decayed and degraded state of moral and patriotic feeling which thinks that nothing is worth war is worse. A man who has nothing for which he is willing to fight; nothing that he cares about more than his own safety; is a miserable creature who has no chance of being free, unless made and kept so by the exertions of better men than himself.
> —John Stuart Mill

That's pretty patriotic. When I was active in the military I felt like that. I guess I still do. I'm still much of a freedom-loving flag waver, and willing to back it up. How about you? Do you have anything for which you are willing to fight?

Core values are those which should be most important in your life...something for which you are willing to fight and die. Well, is there anything for which you are willing to lose your life? For what or whom are you willing to die? That's an even harder question, isn't it? That's a little harder to answer truthfully.

Heck, even the Apostles had trouble with this one. In Matthew (26:35), "Peter said to Him, 'Even if I have to die with You, I will not deny You!' And so said all the disciples." Yeah, boy! Core values. "We'll stick with You, Jesus. We believe in You. We'll die for You (not that it will ever come to that). We won't let them mess with You." Yet, later in the same book, Peter "began to curse and swear, saying 'I do not know the Man!'" (26:74) All of the Apostles bailed out and ran for their lives. For what or whom are you willing to die?

Of course, later they finally found their backbones, again. Then they found that they would die for their beliefs. Indeed, "According to Jerome [one of the early church fathers], Peter was crucified upside down because Peter stated that he was unworthy to be crucified in the same manner as the Lord." Andrew was crucified. Paul was beheaded. Mark was dragged to death. Jude was crucified. Thomas was impaled on a spear, as was Matthew. James the Just was cast from the pinnacle of the Temple, stoned, and bludgeoned with a mallet. They found their core beliefs, and were willing to die for them. For what or whom are you willing to die?

Today, in many, many countries, people are dying for their beliefs. Especially Jews and Christians. Did you know that? Did you realize that there are modern day martyrs? Very true. In today's world there are people who have to choose between their lives and their beliefs…and they are opting to die rather than deny! Amazing!

Now, all but one of you, my correspondents, are living in the United States. We have the freedom and privilege to worship, to believe, however we wish. Maybe that's much of the problem. Because we have the freedom, we don't really have the passion. Perhaps because we never have to choose, we never actually spend much time creating a set of core values by which to live. We never truly generate carefully crafted beliefs to guide our lives.

Have you? Have you taken the time to thoughtfully and prayerfully examine your life and craft a personal mission statement supported by carefully determined beliefs? You've heard all the old saying—IF YOU DON'T KNOW WHERE YOU ARE GOING, HOW WILL YOU EVER GET THERE—or the one from Yogi Berra [which I prefer]—IF YOU DON'T KNOW WHERE YOU'RE GOING WHEN YOU GET THERE YOU WON'T KNOW WHERE YOU ARE.

Really, it's your life. But if your life is going to mean anything at all, don't you need to operate from a plan? Don't you need a set of core beliefs? And if they are worth living, shouldn't they be worth dying for? For what or whom are you willing to die? If your life is to be worth anything, shouldn't there be something? Think about it. Pray about it.

Blessings!

Sunday Musings
9

Beloved,

IN GOD WE TRUST:
ALL OTHERS PAY CASH

That's what the sign by the cash register said when I was a bartender during my freshman year of college. Amusing? Sure. Especially in the '60's in a college town. In a bar. It was the title of a pretty funny book by Jean Shepherd, too. But, you know, I'm afraid that we've reached that point. People just don't trust anymore.

TRUST. My (old) *Webster's New Collegiate* describes it as "1 a: assured reliance on the character, ability, strength, or truth of someone or something." Used to be that we could have "assured reliance" on someone's character or word. Remember when a handshake was sufficient to seal a bargain? We trusted the person to be true to his word. Now it is a sheaf of legal papers, properly notarized and filed. And even then, judging from the lawsuits, it ain't always so. Can't even **TRUST** the legal system to keep someone on the straight-and-narrow. Bummer.

In God is our TRUST. (Francis Scott Key) TRUST *and obey, for there's no other way to be happy, just to* TRUST *and* obey. (John H. Sammis) *Self-*TRUST *is the first secret of success.* (Ralph Waldo Emerson) *Who do you* TRUST? (1950's TV program)

Chris was just remarking to me the other day how sad it is that there is so little trust between husbands and wives, today. Maybe it is the influence of all the television shows that show "wandering" spouses. I don't know. But I guess that's a major part of the reason that the divorce rate hovers around 50%. Of course, in some cases it becomes a self-fulfilling prophecy, too. "Hey, she [or he] doesn't trust me, anyway, so I might just as well do it!" When I perform a wedding ceremony I always make certain to use the passage from Corinthians that says: Love *does not delight in evil, but rejoices with the truth. It always protects, always* TRUSTS, *always hopes, always perseveres.* (1 Corinthians 13) But I guess it doesn't always take. Chris and I have been married for over 33 years, and we **TRUST** each other. I can't imagine any other way to be. If you don't trust…well, the opposite is doubt, or suspect. What a sad way to go through life.

Life is magnificent! I'm a paraplegic, but I can and do believe that. And the reason is, I **TRUST** in God, and God is good—all the time!

And it all starts with God. Of course it does! My belief tells me that He is always there, always listening to my prayers, always concerned about my life. He never allows us more trouble than we can handle, and He is always anxious to help us cope. The skeptic will ask why does He allow *any* trouble to befall those of us who believe and put our **TRUST** in Him? Because it, helps us grow. Heck, even Nietzsche recognized that when he said, "That which does not kill me makes me stronger." Nietzsche wasn't giving God the credit, but that's where it belongs.

So, the next time you wake up don't think, darkly, "Oh, God, it's morning;" think, excitedly, "Thank you, God, it's morning!" Dedicate yourself to enjoying life, and try trusting people. Oh, sure, occasionally you'll be disappointed, but how much better a life is it to **TRUST** God and **TRUST** His people, and go through life expecting the best? You know what? You might find that you actually enjoy living. Next thing you know, you'll be smiling at waitresses and telling the toll-takers on the turnpike to "Have a nice day!" AND MEANING IT! Think about it.

Blessings!

Sunday Musings
10

Beloved,

I received a letter from a friend, a short while ago, asking for…guidance, I guess. Her *significant other* has been diagnosed with cancer, and although he is handling it well, she is not. As she put it, she is "literally falling apart at the seams." This friend is a very intelligent, pragmatic, and successful businesswoman, but she has found that business acumen has not prepared her to deal with this shadowy threat to her well-ordered universe.

World-altering calamities hit all of us, sooner or later—a personal accident, the death of a parent or partner or child, the loss of a job (and security)—we all have to deal with it. Comes the question, "How?" When *life* or *fate* or *karma* finally gets around to dealing us that bad hand, how are we to muddle through? That's what my friend was asking me. She's seen me deal with the death of both parents in just six months, and with the life-changing accident that left me a paralytic. She wanted to know how to handle life's attacks. What I told her is what I want to tell all of you:

> I wish that I had a magic mantra that would make things easier for you, or a talisman that would create a feeling of well-being. I don't. My "magic" is faith. It says in Scripture that we should always be prepared to explain the reason our lives are different—[Peter 3:15] *But sanctify the Lord God in your hearts,* **and always be ready to give a defense to everyone who asks you a reason for the hope that is in you,** *with meekness and fear.*

> THAT is my magic, my mantra, my talisman. When I was initially going through my hospitalization and rehab, there was another Scripture that kept Chris going. She says that when things got bad she would just remember—[Philippians 4:13] *I can do all things through Christ who strengthens me.* It always has been, and continues to be, our faith in our Lord that has seen us through the hard times.

There is a Scripture in Paul's letter to the Romans that says—[Romans 8:28] *And we know that all things work together for good to those who love God, to those who are the called according to His purpose.* In other words, nothing is going to happen to me, ever, that has not first passed through nail-scarred hands. From the first day AFTER my accident I was excited because I figured that God had done this for some reason. I didn't know why…and I am still not certain. BUT, I trust God. He gave me this life and all that I have in it, and it is His to do with as He pleases.

It's a bummer, but the answer to "Why do bad things happen to good people?" is that age-old parental answer—BECAUSE. What works for us Christians is that means BECAUSE GOD SAID SO. Do you remember ever seeing the bumper sticker—GOD SAID IT, I BELIEVE IT, THAT SETTLES IT? That's how I live my life.

It was either Marx or Lenin that said, "Religion is the opiate of the masses." Well, in a good way that's true. I don't allow myself to worry about what's going to happen, or what's happening, because I trust God to do what is right. And as Jesus said, [Matthew 6:27] *Who of you by worrying can add a single hour to his life?*

Sounds a lot easier to say than to do, doesn't it? Well, you have the problem that you live in a world of tangibles. You are used to being able to touch things to believe in them. But to throw all of your problems on Jesus you have to be able to believe in Someone that you will never be able to touch until you meet Him in heaven. That's where faith comes in. Faith is tough. Faith is believing with all your heart in something you cannot touch. [Hebrews 11:1] *Now faith is being sure of what we hope for and certain of what we do not see.* That is tough for modern pragmatic Americans. But there are answers. Some sound glib, but they are true. "How can I possibly believe in or trust something I can't see?" Well, do you breathe? Unless you are living in NYC or L.A. you probably can't see the air you are trusting to keep you alive. Then there is the joke about taking an atheist to a restaurant, treating them to a fine meal, then asking them if they believe there is a cook.

Unfortunately, we try to be too self-sufficient. We are used to "doing it ourselves." Well, it is at times like this that we have to realize that WE CAN'T DO IT ALONE. And when it is something as hugely important as this, our earthly acquaintances can't do it either.

You ask about my "ability to handle life's unexpected events…" It ain't me. The "reason for the hope that is in me" is my faith in Jesus Christ; my belief that, as a Christian, whatever happens to me has first been approved by God; and the fact that I can go to God in prayer.

Prayer is neat! It is the opportunity to actually talk with THE BIG GUY! The One who made all of this. I can just talk with Him, explain how I am feeling, and ask Him to help out.

Will this solve all of our problems? No. We certainly are not promised that when we become Christians we will no longer have sickness or problems. Hey, even Billy Graham has Parkinson's Disease. No, the promise is that when we are in Christ, He will not put anything more on us than we can handle. We'll be stretched, but that will be to deepen our relationship to Him—to force us to allow Him to help get us through.

You can try to struggle on with this in a thinking, pragmatic, worldly fashion, or you can turn it, AND YOURSELF, over to Jesus Christ. That is the way to get through this trial with your personal flags flying. Think about it. PRAY ABOUT IT. And I'll be praying for you.

So, that's what I told my friend. And that's what I am telling you, also. "The reason for the hope that is in me?" *My* total trust in Jesus Christ. I hope that you have that faith already. If you don't, and want to know more about it, just ask! Ask me, or one of your friends who believes in The Way.

As it says in Scripture, [Galatians 5:22]…*the fruit of the Spirit is love, joy, peace, longsuffering, kindness, goodness, [and] faithfulness.* That's a darn great way to go through life. Think about it. Pray about it.

Blessings!

Sunday Musings
11

Beloved,

Do you enjoy irony...as a literary tool? I do. I find it fascinating, and, if I am reading someone's ironic writings (such as Carl Hiaasen), I find it a lot of fun. But, I especially enjoy irony when I am living it in my own life.

I'm just now getting over being ill, again. Actually, the second time in two months. Apart from that not being good physically, this was kind of rough on me psychologically. I get sick of being sick. You know what I mean? And this time I started feeling sorry for myself. Not about being a cripple, just about being sick. Again. And just when I was starting to beat on my chest and say, "Why me," I remembered Betty. Betty is our "adopted" redheaded Cuban daughter—one of my former students with whom we got very close. Betty found out, only about a month ago, that she has Hodgkin's Disease. Cancer of the lymph nodes. Since Betty found out, she has been very up beat. She has turned the entire thing over to the Lord, counting on Him to carry her through. I had a soon-to-be-cured infection. Betty has cancer. I was beginning to feel sorry for myself. Betty was still praising the Lord and being happy. Where did I get off feeling sorry?

But you know what's funny? Ironic? Betty says that what is helping her is (are you ready for this?)—ME. She is gaining strength to handle what she is going through by thinking about how I handled what I went through when I became crippled. So...in my illness I am gaining strength from Betty who in her illness is gaining strength from me in my cripple-ness.

You know what this all really means? It means that all of us—you, me, everyone—are being watched by *someone*, and we are being a model of behavior, for better or worse. Who was it, some professional basketball player, who said that he didn't want to be a role model?

Well, like it or not, we all are. If we have kids, that's obvious. However even if we don't have kids, even if we don't want to be, we are. Someone is watching. Someone is modeling. We don't have a choice, but we do have a responsibility. Once we realize this, then it is time for us to see whom *we* are using as our model. Hmmmmmm. Think about it. Pray about it.

Blessings!

Sunday Musings
12

Beloved,

Remember the song that went,

If you can't be with the one you love, honey,

Love the one you're with.

I have no idea who sang it, but I still remember the tune. The sentiment, then, was free love. Situation ethics. If it feels good, do it. Whomever you are with.

But I'd like to cast it in a different light. I'd like to look at it as saying, *Love Everyone!*

Is that a little too touchy-feely for you? Yeah, I know what you mean. How about that nasty SOB that you work for? Love him!? Or that guy whose dog keeps doing his business in your front yard? Or that slob that cut you off on the way into work on the Interstate this morning? Huh! I showed him. I showed him my...

WHOA! Chill out! Do those things tick you off? Do those people get you stewing so that you are tense and *tetchy* for the rest of the day? Yeah, I know what you mean. Inconsiderate louts. Who do they think...but, wait a minute. If they get *you* angry, and *you* stay angry, and they...well, they don't even know about it. So they're not angry. *Just you.* SON OF A GUN! You know what that means? They win. You lose. Bummer.

That's one reason for not letting things tick you off. Another reason is from the Book of Matthew. In it Jesus is teaching about anger and how everyone is your brother, and He says,

Therefore if you bring your gift to the altar, and there remember that your brother has something against you, leave your gift there before the

altar, and go your way. First be reconciled to your brother, and then come and offer your gift.

He is saying that you can't worship if you are holding something against someone in your heart. In Ephesians Paul writes, *do not let the sun go down on your wrath.* The same idea. You know, it disappoints me when I have some of my students (primarily at FIU) tell me that they feel some of their professors hate teaching and hate their students. What a shame! What a sad way to go through life. These kids are, by and large, wonderful and worth loving, and when we love them it usually comes back. Isn't it that way in your life? When you are nice to someone, aren't they usually nice back to you?

Here's something for those of you who have people that you don't want to love. The Book of Proverbs says,

If your enemy is hungry, give him bread to eat; And if he is thirsty, give him water to drink; For so you will heap coals of fire on his head, And the LORD will reward you.

Huh? That means that if you do nice things for people who don't like you, people who want to "spitefully use" you, it will flummox them. They won't know how to handle it. I used to do that when I was in the Coast Guard. I had one Captain who didn't like me, and who was my boss's boss. I always made it a point to be as nice and friendly and cheerful as possible to him. I pretty much *forced* him to say a nice "hello" to me every day. I knew it hurt his mouth to do so, but it was a lot more fun than my being angry and stewing about how he disliked me. If I let his dislike and disdain make me upset, who was that going to benefit? Not me.

So, *Love the one you're with*—even if he's basically unlovable. It will make your life so much more pleasant. And not only will this remove a heavy burden from your being, but it also makes us available to help others when they hurt or are angry. If we refuse to let anyone be our enemy, then friends constantly surround us. Friends whom we can comfort…and who are there to comfort us, too.

Think about it. Pray about it. And the next time that guy cuts you off on the Interstate, instead of showing him the well-known one-fingered obscene gesture, flash the sign language I LOVE YOU at him, instead. And laugh, good-heartedly.

Blessings!

Sunday Musings
13

Beloved,

Did you put a flag on your car on 9/12, or shortly thereafter? How about on your home? Yeah, we had a real rush of patriotism there for a while. Question: do you still have those flags flying?

After 9/11 everyone was talking about God and talking about prayer in public and religion was suddenly no longer a forbidden topic. Did you talk with friends about how your own spiritual life helped you cope with the aftermath of the disaster? Didn't it feel wonderful to not be afraid to talk about God in public? Question: do you still talk openly about your spiritual beliefs?

It seemed as though people were friendlier immediately after 9/11. Did you notice that? People *wanted* to talk with one another. Not always about the terrorist attacks, either. It just seemed that people wanted more to connect with one another. Did you feel like that? Were you more open in talking with folks whom you didn't necessarily know? Question: are you still friendlier…more open and talking with people?

Americans do seem to rise to the occasion. When there is a disaster, we all pull together. When there are people in need, we will come up with ways of helping them. Why, then, can't we keep it up in between times of calamity?

I can't tell you what to do, how to live your lives. I wouldn't presume to. But for me, I'm continuing to fly my flags. I am continuing to let people know Who it is that helps get me through not just disasters, but every single day. And I am going to continue to smile at strangers, to greet toll takers on the highway, and to be pleasant to store clerks. Joshua 24:15—*But as for me and my house, we will serve the LORD.*

How you live, every day, is your choice. Think about it. Pray about it.

Blessing!

Sunday Musings
14

Beloved,

For those of you who didn't know me back in the '70's [and for those of you who didn't know me all that well], I used to be heavily into photography. I'd shoot a lot of color slides, but I loved shooting in black-and-white. Not "grip-and-grins," though I did shoot enough of those. No, I liked to shoot artistically. I was never very good with a paintbrush, so I used a camera, and amassed quite a file of transparencies and B&W negatives.

What brought this to mind was that Chris gave me a scanner for my birthday that allows me to scan negatives and slides into my computer. Back when I originally shot this stuff I had a pretty extensive darkroom where I'd spend hours processing and printing. All of my darkroom equipment is in boxes in the garage, now, but technology allows me to do on my computer virtually everything I formerly did in my darkroom. It's great. I'm getting photographically oriented again.

Where am I headed with all of this? When I was carrying a camera with me everywhere I went, I trained myself to see everything through a photographer's eye. I don't mean thinking about *f*-stops and shutter speeds. What I would do was try to continually frame attractive photographs as I went through my day. I can remember, for instance, looking at an old building and not noticing the building as much as how the skeletal fire escape zigzagged its way from the top to the bottom. When the city put up a new communications tower I didn't look it as much from the outside as a tower as I did standing directly beneath it and looking at the high-contrast design of concentric triangles that it made.

When I'd go deer hunting, I would make it a point to frame at least five GOOD pictures wherever I sat. I wouldn't shoot them, necessarily, but I was training myself to *see* instead of just *look*. City Hall had two ficus trees planted in the lobby. They were pretty enough, but what was *truly* artistically beautiful was the interlocking matrix of exposed roots they exhibited.

OK. So what? Well, here's what—how often during the day do you *not see* some example of God's beauty? Well, sure, sunrises and sunsets are kind of obvious. God's not real subtle with them. Down here, in Florida, they fairly scream LOOK AT HOW BEAUTIFUL I AM! Have you ever looked at the way a flower blossom is put together—all overlapped and interwoven? Have you ever taken a single leaf and turned it over and looked at the fascinating pattern of veins and capillaries on its bottom? Have you ever looked at the diaphanous wings of a dragonfly, or the iridescent glow of its body? Have you ever picked up a pinecone and really *looked* at it? You can't do that without being amazed and appreciative.

A radio preacher I heard this morning was urging us on to more prayer and praise in our lives. I guess most of us are good at prayer…especially when things are going wrong. Well, I suppose we aren't too bad at praying and thanking God when we have something particularly good happen to us. But we need to be praising Him constantly, every time we see another of His wonders in creation. Whenever we take the time to recognize the beauty of the commonplace all around us, we need to soak it in, and thank The One who provided it for our appreciation. I know He'd appreciate hearing how much we enjoy it. Think about it. Pray about it.

Blessings!

Sunday Musings
15

Beloved,

Now, don't get me wrong. I love our country and I love the society in which we live. We certainly are not all that we can be, but we sure have come a long way [baby] from where we were. And we are getting better all the time. HOWEVER [you just knew that was coming, didn't you?], we do have some problems, and I want to look at one for just a quick moment.

In preparation for a class at Trinity International University I am again reading *FIRST THINGS FIRST*, by Steven Covey. In the book Covey mentions "the quick-fix illusion." It something from which most all of us Americans suffer.

Consider: those of us from the baby boom generation and younger have been brought up on solving most problems in 30 or 60-minutes [with time out for commercials]. Much of our *reality* is based around television, where entire calm-to-crisis-to-conclusion takes only enough time to fit the slot available for it. We are used to life-changing events being resolved in time for the nightly news. We get used to thinking in terms of the "quick-fix."

Our entire lives get to be that way. We have microwave dinners, abridged editions, fast food restaurants, Cliff's Notes, READER'S DIGEST, quickie divorces, express lanes at the grocery store, and so forth. We kind of forget what real life is all about. When we get to school, instead of "wasting" time studying, we try to take the quick-fix there, and just "cram" the course. "Goof off all semester, then spend all night before the big test trying to cram a semester's worth of learning into [our] head[s]." It might work for the short run, but you haven't learned anything for life. It's just a "quick-fix." And, you know, it's all tied up with principles. How? Follow me:

Covey talks about the "Law of the Farm [which] governs in all arenas of life." THE LAW OF THE FARM? Yes—can you imagine not bothering to take the time to plow and plant in the spring, being busy with other things all summer, and then in the fall frantically trying to PLANT-AND-WATER-AND-WEED-AND-FERTILIZE and expect to have something ready to harvest virtually overnight? Doesn't work that way. As brilliant as you might be, you can't "cram" farming. That's the "Law of the Farm." It differentiates between a social system and a natural system. A social system is one that is, essentially, "made up." Oh, it might be well thought through by learned minds, but it is still a creation of someone's mind, while a natural system…is. No individual created it, it just…is.

As Covey says, "what about character? Can you 'cram' and suddenly become a person of integrity, courage, or compassion?" Well, sure, but there are other areas where that doesn't really count, right? There are areas where quick-fixes work, aren't there?

Actually, I can't think of any that matter. How about raising kids? Chris and Jennifer were talking about the teaching profession, last night, about how parents try to shift responsibility for teaching morals and behavior and life-skills to the schools. There's the quick-fix mentality, and it doesn't work. In an effort to "quick-fix" it parent abrogate their responsibilities, and end up with mal-adjusted kids.

Well, then, how about something as mundane as training a dog. We're bigger and smarter, and we can forcibly impose our will, right? Sure, and what does our quick-fix give us? A broken spirit.

It's a bummer for the intelligentsia, but there *are* immutable principles by which the world operates. They can't be socially engineered, and they can't be relativistically modified. They just *are*.

Those of us of the Judeo-Christian persuasion know why they are, and where they came from. We may try to ignore them, or get around them, or modify them to our own ends, but deep down inside we know Who set them up that way, and why we won't be able to change them.

So, are you stuck in the "quick-fix illusion?" Are you caught wondering why your speedy solutions to problems don't hold up under scrutiny or fire? Are you constantly making up your mind that "this is the way it is going to be," only to find out that "this is the way that it is?" Maybe it's time that you stopped looking for the quick-fix, slowed down for a minute, and really considered what the laws of nature are, why they are immutable, and Who said so. Think about it.

Blessings!

Sunday Musings
16

Beloved,

We talked about love in Sunday School. The text was 1 John 4:7-21. We discussed how God actually was the One to initiate love for us, and that His love is unconditional. No matter what we do wrong [and believe me, we do a lot], God is going to love us. It's like the bumper sticker I have cited before that says,

GOD LOVES YOU WHETHER YOU WANT HIM TO OR NOT

I love that!

We then went on to see that God's love is manifested in us. :21, *And this commandment we have from Him: that he who loves God must love his brother also.* If we love God, then we have to love others. Kind of like the "Golden Rule," isn't it? "Do unto others…"

In our small group this lead to a discussion of attitudes. How we look at others and react to others and feel about others all depends on our attitude. If we are in a good mood, have a good attitude, then we might not react as negatively when that guy cuts in front of us on the interstate. If, however, we have been going through the day chewing up ten-penny nails and spitting out carpet tacks, when he cuts in front of us we are going to go ballistic! Right? Either way what the other guy did was the same. It's not him. IT'S US! WE decide how we are going to react. WE decide whether we are going to just blow it off, or try to blow him off the road. WE decide whether we are going to "do unto others *as* we would have them do unto us," or "*before* they can do it to us."

I do not like getting up in the morning. I used to. Before I got crippled I enjoyed being the first one up. I loved the quiet outdoors before the sunrise, with the birds just beginning to stir. No more. Now getting up in the morning is physically difficult because of my disabilities.

HOWEVER, if I let that affect my attitude, if I allow my early-morning struggle cloud up my entire day, then who loses? ME!

> *Well, sure, that's easy for you to say. But did you see what that SOB did?!*
>
> *Yes, he cut you off, and made you slam on your brakes and spill your coffee in your lap. I can understand why you are angry. But, is the guy who cut you off angry?*
>
> *No.*
>
> *Does he even know that you are back here sending thunderbolts of furious psychic anger at him, trying to disrupt his karma?*
>
> *No.*
>
> *Then who won? If he is blissfully unaware of anything being awry, and you're back here with your ulcer getting ready to erupt...who is the winner? HE IS!!!!!*

Don't let others control your happiness...your attitude. It's yours. When you wake up in the morning, decide,

> *This is another of the very few days I have allotted to me. I'm going to enjoy it.*

For those of you of an evangelical bent, just sing,

> This is the day,
> This is the day
> That the Lord has made,
> That the Lord has made.

> I will rejoice,
> I will rejoice
> And be glad in it,
> And be glad in it.

Really, the choice *is* up to you. Think about it.

Blessings!

Sunday Musings
17

Beloved,

MIRACLES ON A MOUNTAINSIDE!

That's what they called last week at Snowmass Village, Aspen, Colorado. The reason was the 313 disabled U.S. veterans—paraplegics, quadriplegics, vision impaired, MS, amputees, stroke—were all proving that they were not un-abled, but simply differently-abled. It was amazing…and motivating.

Have you ever skied? You know the terror you felt when you first went flying down the slope? Think about doing that BLIND! Consider: Chuck is a young quadriplegic who broke his neck in a diving accident. Chuck is a pretty high level quad, and has just the least little bit of ability to move his right arm. Chuck was strapped into a mono-ski, which is a fiberglass seat or cockpit mounted on a single ski. After some simple lessons, an instructor (there were 165 volunteer instructors who paid their own way to participate) took him up the slope on the chairlift. The instructor had a tether attached to Chuck's mono-ski, and they flew down the slope together. Chuck was ecstatic!

I guess one of the most important things about the 16th Winter Sports Clinic was that it gave us a chance to again do something which we were able to do before we became disabled—that and to prove to others and ourselves that we are not helpless cripples. We are able. Just differently. We live in a new reality, and just must cope with our new lot in life.

I wish that you could have seen the crazy people out there. Chris remarked that she was simply amazed by the attitudes of the participants. There weren't any who were in self-pity parties. They all seemed to have fully accepted their disability, realizing that there isn't anything they can do about it, and are getting on with their lives. It makes you reconsider the problems in your own life. I saw a man completely paralyzed from the chest down climb a 25' high rock wall. How? They strapped him into a harness attached to a locking pulley system. He was then able to pull with his arms and ratchet himself up to the top. I saw blind climbers do the same by feel. I climbed the rock, with an able-bodied (AB) climber below me helping me get my foot up to occasional footholds when my muscles wouldn't do it. [I have never been so tired as when I finally got back down!]

Miracles on the Mountainside! There were people with no legs at all cross-country skiing. There were amputees riding handcycles. There were blind participants fly-casting. There were paraplegics playing sled hockey. They refused to accept their handicaps as disabilities, just different abilities.

What's your disability? Is it a negative attitude? Or a poor memory? Or a job that you feel is less than you deserve? Or a spouse that you feel should be more understanding? Or a bad hair day? Are you letting it *cripple* you? You know, it's up to you. You set your own limits. You decide the degree of *dis-* of your *ability*. Are you going to sit there and mope, or get out and do? Think about it.

Blessings!

Sunday Musings
18

Beloved,

Florida Power & Light has a TV commercial that asks, "What do you live for?" The "reporter" goes on the street and asks the question of people who reply; "I live to ride, Bob" (a Harley rider) or, "I live to fish," or, "For my wife." (Newlywed, of course.) I think that the gist is that FP&L lives to supply us with inexpensive electricity, though any student who has studied under me in a business class knows what the real *raison d'etre* of a corporation is—all together now, "TO MAKE A PROFIT FOR THE STOCKHOLDERS."

Anyway, in spite of the commercial, it's a good question: What do you live for? If the answer is, "My family," or, "My wife," that's not too bad. Is that true, or are you just trying to stay out of trouble? We'll see.

A tried-and-true way of seeing what you live for is to look at your checkbook. Certainly your mortgage is where you spend your most money [at least, I hope it is], but where else does your money go? What is the first check that you write each month? That's one way of telling. What do you live for?

Another method involves your answering two simple questions: 1) When you are sitting daydreaming, to what do your thoughts gravitate? 2) When you have some "extra" money when the bills have been paid, on what do you spend it? The answer to these two questions, along with that one about where your first check goes, will give you a good idea of what is most important in your life—what you live for. What do you live for?

A lot of years ago I wrote a little piece about guys who live for their vehicles...or in this case, their pickup trucks. You know the ones. They have the bumper sticker that says I LOVE MY TRUCK. You can see that their truck is the recipient of their spare time and spare money. (I wonder if they realize that it starts depreciating the minute they drive it off the lot?) What do you live for?

I'm up on the Chesapeake Bay, right now, and [to my south Florida mind] it's cold. The air is in the 60's, and a brisk breeze is blowing. But one thing I wanted to do, this vacation, was to copy the notes I've taken in my NIV-translation Bible into my New King James. It's nice, sitting on the enclosed front porch, looking out at the whitecaps in The Bay, doing this kind of task, and it enabled me to re-discover an important passage in Deuteronomy, called the "Shema." De 6:4-9 *"Hear, O Israel: The LORD our God, the LORD is one! You shall love the LORD your God with all your heart, with all your soul, and with all your strength. And these words which I command you today shall be in your heart. You shall teach them diligently to your children, and shall talk of them when you sit in your house, when you walk by the way, when you lie down, and when you rise up. You shall bind them as a sign on your hand, and they shall be as frontlets between your eyes. You shall write them on the doorposts of your house and on your gates."* In other words, the Lord is commanding us, all of us, to make the Lord the center of our lives. HE is the one that we are to live for.

Wouldn't it be wonderful if our lives, if everyone's lives, were centered around church and belief in God? That's the way it used to be. Everyone worshipped on the Sabbath, the church was the center of social lives, and even government realized that there was Someone more powerful than they. Someone to whom *they* were responsible.

Is it archaic of me to wish that we all would live the beliefs we profess? Think about it, and while you're at it, think about what you live for.

Blessings!

Sunday Musings
19

Beloved,

Are you creative? I don't know if I believe that everyone has some variety of creativity in them—probably so, because there are so many different kinds. Back when I was selling decorated glass in the furniture industry I had a boss who told me that I was uncreative because I could not come up with artistic designs for the glass. I thought that I was creative because I could write pretty good copy. I also was very creative in some of the photography that I was doing. I had painted, too, although I had to have a picture to copy—I couldn't just create one from my mind.

Are you an artist? Something I was reading in a management book the other day really hit me—we are all artists in what we do with our days. When we awake in the morning we are artists preparing to create either a masterpiece or a mess. Which do you want to create? It's up to you, you know.

I know! You've heard my "it's your choice" talk before. Well, I want to take four lessons from the book *FISH!*, a book about work, and tell you how we can apply it to our everyday lives.

The first lesson is, *Choose your own attitude.* Yes, you have heard that before, but unless you choose to enjoy life, every day of it, and choose to blow off the negative stuff, then the rest of it just won't work. Easy for me to say? Well, yes, it is, but only because I have refused to invest too much in being a victim. For too many people being a victim is their life's goal. That way they can have pity parties, and always blame someone or something else for any problems they encounter. They have created prisons for themselves, and the walls are their own lack of self-confidence. Don't whine to me about your job or your disabilities or your kids or your bad-hair-day, or that if only you had this one's brains or that one's good looks. Pearl Bailey once said, "God doesn't make no mistakes." He made us in His own image, and with all of the looks and brains and ability that we need to fulfill His goals for us in life. So, get over the breast-beating, and *Choose your own attitude.*

The second lesson is, *Play.* As I said this book is written about work. We can choose to enjoy whatever work it is that we do. My father used to say that *it's not doing what you like but liking what you do,* and there is a lot of truth in that. Sometimes, much of the time, we can't get jobs doing what we really want to do. There are just so many professional bass fishermen or models or racecar drivers. Someone has to be the one doing the paperwork, but we can enjoy doing it. It's kind of like when I was in basic training in the Army. I didn't really like it, but I knew that I didn't have a choice, so I made the most of it and enjoyed what and where I could. When I had one boring job in the Coast Guard, I used to engage my troops in rubber band battles in the middle of the workday. Not a big thing, perhaps, but it was *Play.* We can *Play* in whatever we do during the day. HAVE FUN, for pity's sake!

Lesson three: *Make their day.* Engage those around us in our play. If we can share the enjoyment we have in our lives then life and work becomes one big adult playground. Wouldn't you rather be living and working in a playland than a prison?

The final lesson is *Be Present.* Be *with* those you interact with everyday. It may be co-workers or our kids or our spouse or all of the above. *Be present* with them, and they will be for us. Listen to them actively, not while reading the paper or watching the TV or talking on the phone. Engage them in our activities because we want to. Especially with our kids, remember that they are only on loan to us for a short time and then will be leaving.

Jesus promised us that He came to bring us life and more abundantly. It is up to us to open ourselves to accept the gift. Everyday. Everywhere. Always. To do otherwise is to reject a gift directly from God. Think about it.

Blessings!

Sunday Musings
20

Beloved,

They've been replaying **APOLLO 13** on television lately. Isn't what we've done in space exploration amazing? Actually leaving human footprints on the moon! Wow! [I'll bet my Mom wished that they had swept up after themselves.] Science is just phenomenal. We've created strains of wheat and corn that fight off pests on their own without the help of insecticides. We have figured out how to take the mucky sludge left over from pre-historic plants rotting and refine it into fuels. Human ingenuity. We have even been able to take something like the diamond, a crystal that nature has taken centuries and huge physical powers to create, and crafted them easily enough to produce them commercially. We've gone jewelry diamonds one better—we've created artificial diamonds that are clearer and "sparklier" than the real thing at a fraction of the cost. Just amazing. On the medical side we've been able to build a mechanical pump that can, for a period of time, take the place of a person's natural heart. Unbelievable! We've extended lives, and increased the quality of those lives on a massive scale. We haven't actually *created* life, yet, but keep watching.

Maybe that's why. We are so impressed with our own powers and capabilities that we haven't left a lot of room for the indefinable, for God. We've now got the Hubble Telescope that can look unfathomable miles into space, and electron microscopes that can show us the smallest particles imaginable, and we've created them. It was the mind of man that took the problem and formulated the answer. We are able to put most anything we want into a "box" of rationality. Maybe that's why so many people, today, have trouble with the concept of a totally unbound, unboxed, un-quantifiable God. If we can't wrap our minds around something, then it must not actually be. Right?

This concept first came to me as I was flying over the Rocky Mountains. Man can do so much. Scientists can do so much more than you or I can even contemplate. It's pretty impressive. Until you consider something like the Rockies. Have you ever seen the Rockies? They are vast…majestic…awesome…magnificent. Kind of like God. Oh, sure, nuclear fission or animal cloning might be fabulously difficult, but man's mind, some man's mind, can understand them. But who can truly understand the Rocky Mountains—their massive creation—their grandeur—their virtually incomprehensible beauty? Rather puts us in our place.

In his trilogy, *HITCHIKER'S GUIDE TO THE GALAXY*, Douglas Adams postulates the horrifying "Total Perspective Vortex." When placed in it a person is suddenly shown *in one instant the whole infinity of creation and herself in relation to it.* It is said that *the shock completely annihilate[s] [the] brain,* because suddenly you realize that creation is…well, really big and you [and I] are, well, really miniscule. Kind of like when pseudo-intelligentsia tries to think about God, and decide that He couldn't exist because He'd be soooooo much bigger than they.

The Rockies. They are so colossal that a man simply can't personally relate to them. Kind of like life and death and forever and eternity, so overwhelming that man can't personally relate to them. Kind of like God the Creator, so overwhelming and huge that man can't personally relate to Him. Guess that's why Jesus, God-made-man, had to come—someone with whom we could identify. Think about it.

Blessings!

Sunday Musings
21

Beloved,

There's a fascinating little book I use in one of my classes at Trinity International University. It's entitled *In the Name of Jesus* by Fr. Henri Nouwen.[1] Now, you Jewish friends who get this letter don't tune out yet. This is not a theological polemic. Read on.

Nouwen is a learned man. He was *a teacher of pastoral psychology, pastoral theology, and Christian spirituality* at Harvard, and had been a priest for twenty-five years. But feeling burned out, he left Harvard and went to work at L'Arche, a community for mentally handicapped people. Nouwen writes:

> So I moved from Harvard to L'Arche, from the best and the brightest, wanting to rule the world, to men and women who had few or no words and were considered, at best, marginal to the needs of our society.

> The first thing that struck me when I came to live in a house with mentally handicapped people was that their liking or disliking me had absolutely nothing to do with any of the many useful things I had done until then. Since nobody could read my books, they could not impress anyone, and since most of them never went to school, my twenty years at Notre Dame, Yale, and Harvard did not provide a significant introduction.

> I was suddenly faced with my naked self, open for affirmations and rejections, hugs and punches, smiles and tears, all dependent simply on how I was perceived at the moment. In a way, it seemed as though I was starting my life all over again. Relationships, connections, reputations could no longer be counted on...it forced me to rediscover my true identity.

---

1.   Nouwen, Henri J.M. <u>In the Name of Jesus</u>, 1997. NY: The Crossroad Publishing Company.

I have a hard time wrapping my mind around the concept of *my naked self,* the essential *me.* Not Professor Wilson, nor the Rev. Wilson, nor LCDR Wilson. Not Chris' husband nor Rachel and Jonathan's father. Not the university graduate of High Point and Maryland. Not the owner of the house on the lake or the cottage on the Chesapeake Bay. Just my unadorned self. Like you, I pretty much describe myself by things I have done or things I am doing now.

Think about how much of your self-image is defined by your education or your accomplishments or your position or your belongings. Now consider yourself devoid of all of that. This is how God sees you. He isn't impressed with the initials tacked after your name, or your bank balance, or your title. All He cares about is the inner you…your core being…your essence. Consider what He does. Is your core being up to the divine scrutiny? Think about it. Pray about it.

Blessings!

Sunday Musings
22

Beloved,

Wow! It's been a long time since I've written on Sunday. I'm sorry. As most of you know, it's because I was in Ohio training with and receiving a service dog. Now I'm home with Alex, a black Labrador retriever, and things are slowly getting back to normal.

I got a really humbling e.mail this week from one of my students. It was anonymous, and I don't recognize the address. Part of what it said was: *I came home from your class tonight with an incredible feeling, as I always do after your lectures. I have never met anyone with such an incredible amount of happiness and such a strong desire to spread good will.* WOW! Can you begin to imagine how wonderful that makes me feel?

So, what do I do in class to engender such a reaction? Nothing special. It's just that I teach because I truly love my students, each and every one of them, and I try to teach them more than just the academic subjects assigned. I try to teach them about life, and how to appreciate it. I'm only an adjunct professor, a part-time instructor, but I see it as an opportunity to minister to these wonderful students. I have no real authority or really any expertise, but I look at teaching as a way to have fun and help others. I guess it is working.

What is it that you do for a living? Do you interact with others? When they come away from meeting with you, do they feel better for the experience? It's really up to you. I'm certainly nothing special, but when I wake up in the morning I realize that I have a choice—I can choose to be happy, or I can choose to be grumpy. Through the pre-coffee cobwebs and half-opened eyes, I choose to be happy. When something untoward happens to me, like getting cut off in traffic or having the toll-taker not understand about my disabled toll permit, I can choose to get angry, or I can choose to blow it off and stay happy. I choose to stay happy. Heck, when I was lying paralyzed from the neck down in the neurological intensive care unit at Mercy Hospital I could choose to beat my breast (figuratively) and cry "Why me?" or I could choose to say, "Well, it's happened, I accept it, what's next?" I chose to stay happy.

Eleanor Roosevelt said something to the effect that no one can belittle you without your permission. Well, similarly, you must give yourself permission to be angry or sad. Or you can give yourself permission, every day, to be happy and uplifting. And if you do, then life will be so much better and enjoyable not only for you, but for everyone who comes in contact with you.

So, which is it going to be? When you wake up tomorrow morning, pause for a moment. You can either say "Thank you, God, its Monday!" Or, you can groan, "Oh, God, its Monday." The choice is yours, but it will stay with you throughout the day. Think about it. Pray about it.

Blessings!

Sunday Musings
23

Beloved,

You all know about my service dog, Alex. Let me tell you something new:

Assistance Dogs of America, Inc. (ADAI), the organization who trained Alex, only uses dogs they rescue from shelters, dogs donated by the occasional breeder, or pets that are being surrendered by the owners because they either don't want them or can't handle them. Alex was a shelter dog. He was at the Toledo Humane Society when one of trainers from ADAI came by to evaluate the dogs at the shelter for their potential to become service dogs. I think it was Mechele who fortunately found Alex and decided he was worth giving a chance. Alex was big and rambunctious. He liked to show his excitement by jumping up, which can be rather off-putting with a jet-black 75-pound beast. Alex probably was not easily adoptable, and quite possibly would have been destroyed. At that time, Alex was virtually worthless. Then ADAI took him. After all of his training, Alex is now worth about $15,000.

Isn't that amazing? Once Alex was a candidate for destruction; now he is worth almost as much as my first house cost! Actually, his value was always there. It just took someone to see it and bring it out of him.

Isn't that the same as it is with so many people? At first glance they might not look like much—they might seem dumb or dirty or disorganized or disreputable. But if you take the time to look more closely you realize that they all do have something to offer.

I've often thought or wondered or worried that about the myriad homeless we have in south Florida. To look at them now they are dirty and smelly. Some would call them the dregs of humanity. But at one time they were cute little babies. Someone, *someone,* loved them once upon a time. At one time they had positive potential. And they are all made in God's image, no matter how grubby they may appear to our human eyes.

I suppose what I am getting at is: Who are we to judge? Better we should have sympathy, feel compassion, and, at the very least, pray. Because, really, "there but for fortune, or the grace of God, go you and I." Think about it. Pray about it.

Blessings!

Sunday Musings
24

Beloved,

Her name is Annette. She is an outdoorsy-person. She owns horses and dogs and other animals, and her profession is dog trainer. As a matter of fact, Annette was one of the primary trainers of Alex, my service dog. She is very special to me.

Annette was driving home last Thursday night and fell asleep at the wheel of her pickup truck. I guess she woke up when the wheels went off the side of the road, and she over-corrected. The truck went out-of-control, rolled several times, and just like that Annette became a C6 quadriplegic. She does not have any feeling from chest down (I can identify with that), and no feeling in her hands. She can move her arms, and a little bit of her wrists. She will be in a halo for three months because of the cervical fracture and because all of her neck ligaments were stretched or torn.

Why am I telling you this? Two reasons. The first is that, if you believe that way, I'd ask you to pray for Annette and her family. If your church has an active prayer chain, ask them to pray for her, too. Remember:

> *James 5:15-16 And the prayer of faith will save the sick, and the Lord will raise him up…pray for one another, that you may be healed. The effective fervent prayer of a righteous man avails much.*

The second reason is to remind you…STUFF HAPPENS! Every day the unexpected happens to the unprepared, and life is never the same. What will you do if you are the next one? How will you handle it? How will you cope? Or will you?

As you know, I try to make this weekly letter spiritual without beating you over the head with my Bible, but when something this big happens, I can't not say it—God will help you get through these things. Your strength is not sufficient. *His* strength and grace is. When I was in the hospital, it was Philippians 4:13 that enabled Chris to get through all of the rough times. It reads: *I can do all things through Christ who strengthens me.*

And although it is almost a cliché, I held onto Romans 8:28: *And we know that all things work together for good to those who love God, to those who are the called according to His purpose.* For those of you who want to put it off until later, there is always the line about not wanting to be planning on getting saved on Friday, but being called before the Throne on Wednesday.

People, it can happen to you. Please, be ready. And while you are living your life, remember to work like you don't need the money, love like you've never been hurt, and dance like no one is looking. God gave us this life to enjoy to its fullest. Do so while He allows it. Think about it.

Blessings!

Sunday Musings
25

Beloved,

For those of you praying, Annette was moved to a rehab hospital, but at present there is no change in her condition.

<><   <><   ><

I suppose that it's normal for all of us to hear of an accident like Annette's and ask, "What if?" Who hasn't asked that question? What if...I had done things a different way? "What if?" What if Annette hadn't gotten up so early that morning so that she wouldn't have been so sleepy driving home from the Mudhens game? What if she had left the game early...or decided not to go because it was too hot? "What if?"

The problem is that "What if" just creates a false premise in our minds. It postulates that something else might have happened which would have had a presumably better outcome for us. It is a great thing for those of us who like to write fiction, but it just doesn't help living in the real world. *Real* world. *Reality.* What a concept! Our challenge is not to dream about what might have been.

That's a little of what I will be talking about this weekend. On Saturday I have the honor of being a keynote speaker at a spiritual retreat here, in south Florida, speaking on "Going Through The Fire," a trip that all of us make, to one degree or another. Oh, we might not have as severe an accident as Annette, but we all have our times. We all get singed.

You can never tell how someone will react when they find themselves in that sort of situation. While preparing for my talk I've been thinking a fair amount about that. When something like this happens, it creates a "new reality" for an individual. You do have your memories, your yesterdays; but your "now" world changes. Now you have to decide whether you are going to strive against the fates, or accept your life, as modified, and persevere.

We all have drastic changes in our lives. Though when observed dispassionately these changes may, for the most part, seem less drastic than paralysis, when observed from the point of the recipient, or victim, they are every bit as devastating. The death of a beloved pet—or a beloved parent. Breaking a precious piece of china—or a precious leg. Crashing your computer—or your car. *Your* problem *is* the *most difficult in the world* while *you* have to deal with it. How will you deal with it? I guess the answer to that is closely tied up with character, and belief, and spirituality, and strength...

Do you have problems, a new reality with which you must deal? What do *you* have to do? The choice really is yours. You can beat your breast, shake your fist at the heavens, and cry out, "Why me?" Or you can say, "Well, here's where I am. Here's what I've got. What do I do now?" Oh! And if you want to do it really right—PRAY!

I have a little plaque that says, "We can't change the wind, but we can adjust our sails." We can't change our reality, but we can learn to live within it. To cope. To overcome. To succeed. And I'll guarantee you, asking for His help in dealing with our realities is the easiest way to go. Try it.

Blessings!

Sunday Musings
26

Beloved,

I just started reading *Imitation of Christ* by Thomas à Kempis. I've a wonderful translation of it on my computer. Right at the beginning I was struck by a passage:

> …it is not learning that makes a man holy and just, but a virtuous life makes him pleasing to God. I would rather feel contrition than know how to define it. For what would it profit us to know the whole Bible by heart and the principles of all the philosophers if we live without grace and the love of God?

You know what that means? We can be smart as a whip, know all sorts of things, have all sorts of degrees, but if we don't know how to *live,* how to apply our knowledge, what good is it? For my Florida International University secular humanists, if you have all the money in the world, but are still unsatisfied, what good has it done you?

> It is vanity, therefore, to seek and trust in riches that perish. It is vanity also to court honor and to be puffed up with pride. It is vanity to follow the lusts of the body and to desire things for which severe punishment later must come. It is vanity to wish for long life and to care little about a well-spent life. It is vanity to be concerned with the present only and not to make provision for things to come. It is vanity to love what passes quickly and not to look ahead where eternal joy abides.

Remember the book by Joseph Heller, *Catch-22*? One of the characters is afraid to die, so spends his time trying to be as bored as possible so that times seems to creep by. Doesn't say much for the quality of his life, just its length. His priorities were skewed.

How are our priorities? If we have a little extra time, do we spend it on the computer (or watching television), or with our kids or wives? If we have a little extra money after paying the bills do we splurge on ourselves, or do we donate to charity or our church so that it's value can be multiplied and spread around? Do we spend extra hours working, to earn more money, but don't have the time to enjoy it with our families? We *know* how we should live our lives. Do we live what we know? Think about it. Pray about it.

Blessings!

Appendix A

Up From The Depths

January 1993

I'd like to tell you a story about myself:

> *Job 2:4-6 So Satan answered the Lord and said, "Skin for skin! Yes, all that a man has he will give for his life. But stretch out Your hand now, and touch his bone and his flesh, and he will surely curse You to Your face!" And the Lord said to Satan, "Behold, he is in your hand, but spare his life."*

Life looked pretty good in July of 1992. On the first of the month I had received my long-awaited promotion to Lieutenant Commander in the Coast Guard. I had also received orders for a transfer out of south Florida, and we were now looking forward to a move up north. We had sold our home in Ft. Lauderdale, bought a new three-story one in Maryland, the movers had come to make their initial evaluation, and on the twenty-fifth we would be driving north. Or so we had planned before the Lord allowed our plans to be changed.

On July 11th, just two weeks before we were to start our drive to Annapolis, my son, Jonathan, and I went for our last pre-move scuba diving trip together. Jonathan was heading off to the Air Force in October, and we wanted to have some time together before we moved and he left. We decided to take a deep dive on the CGC Duane, a former Coast Guard cutter that was now sunk in 130 feet of water as part of the artificial reef system off Key Largo, the northernmost of the Florida Keys. Jonathan and I were both experienced divers. He is a dive supervisor, and I had been a diving instructor for four years with more than two hundred dives to my credit. We were experienced, we were careful. It wasn't enough.

The dive went well. It was a beautiful day, the water was warm with good visibility, there were many schools of barracuda and baitfish in and around the wreck, and we enjoyed our brief bottom time. On the way to the surface, as we made our safety stop at fifteen feet, my right arm felt a little numb, but I didn't recognize the symptom. What was happening was the onset of decompression sickness...the "bends." Though I didn't realize it at the time, I was also getting a "hit" of nitrogen bubbles in my cerebral cortex, and my thinking was becoming muddled. I remember thinking that the numbness in my arm must be due to my wetsuit sleeve being too tight and cutting off my circulation. Once we got to the surface, I had trouble swimming to the dive boat. I couldn't seem to grasp the lifeline tossed to us by the captain. I felt unreasonably tired and weak, and couldn't even climb up onto the dive platform at the stern of the boat, and had to be pulled aboard. As the captain pulled me up onto the platform I saw my right arm flopping around, totally flaccid. Then things started to deteriorate quickly. As more nitrogen bubbles started to form in my spine and my brain I lost my ability to speak. I lay in the bottom of the boat trying to make words come out to reassure my son that I was OK, but I couldn't seem to make my mouth form the words. As Jonathan held my hand I lapsed into unconsciousness.

For reasons known only to him the dive boat captain did not call the nearby Coast Guard station for help. Instead he called his dive shop and the Pennekamp Coral Reef State Park Patrol, reporting that he had a "sick" diver on board—he didn't identify it as a diving acci-dent—and decided to run me in to an ambulance at the dock in the boat.

I was barely conscious when we arrived, and the EMS personnel worked on me in the ambulance, both at the dock and on the way to a local hospital, for about a half-hour. I remember them telling me to "stay with them," as I again tried and failed to speak. But, then, once they got the oxygen mask on me and an IV started, I felt better. By the time I got to the hospital I was conscious, lucid, and very embarrassed! Here I was a diving instructor causing all this trouble! All that I wanted was for them to release me, let me get in my van and drive home. I could move my legs and arms; I felt fine. "Let me go home!" But, no, the doctor insisted that I go to a hyperbaric chamber for decompression. Well, he was the doctor. The ER personnel assured me that an ambulance would be there momentarily to drive me to the chamber in Miami. So I lay there and waited. And waited. And waited.

Those who have had any diving instruction know that speed is of the essence in treating diving accidents. For reasons that I won't go into here it was six hours between my accident and when I finally was delivered to the hyperbaric chamber at Mercy Hospital in Miami.

At Mercy Hospital they wheeled me into the Emergency Room and began to poke and prod. They explained that they were going to put me into the decompression chamber, and explained all that would happen. They gave me a clipboard with a release form on it, and asked me to sign, but I couldn't seem to get my arms and hands to work, no matter how hard I tried. I could just barely hold the pen, but managed to scratch something on the line. Then they asked me to shift over to a stretcher that would go into the chamber, but I was unable to do so. They pulled me onto the stretcher and then placed me in the decompression chamber.

At that time the chamber at Mercy was a steel cylinder large enough for three seated people. It was only about four feet in diameter, so if you could climb in, you had to do so in a crouch. In my case, they had to squeeze me in on that narrow stretcher. My back had been strained when they pulled me into the dive boat, and my lower back kept spasming painfully while I lay on the almost-unpadded stretcher. Once in the chamber they pressurized it to an equivalent of being sixty feet under water, and I breathed pure oxygen through an uncomfortable rubber mask. The people who ran the chamber kept telling me that this mask was the same as is used by fighter pilots, but I wasn't impressed. It was hard to breathe, and I had to struggle to suck air into my lungs. I was tired. I was sick. I was uncomfortable. And now I couldn't breathe. Thank goodness I wasn't claustrophobic, also! Throughout my time in the chamber the "tender" who was with me kept taking my vital signs, and tried to get me to move my extremities. He also used a sharp instrument to test where I had feeling and where I was without sensation. I was too disoriented to realize it, then, but I wasn't moving much, and had no feeling below my upper chest. My first session in the hyperbaric chamber at Mercy Hospital lasted six hours.

In ninety-two percent of decompression sickness cases the patient comes out of the hyperbaric chamber almost healed. There might still be a little spotty numbness or some little muscular problems, but essentially it is a seemingly miraculous cure. When they pulled my stretcher out of the chamber they brought in a wheelchair and asked me to climb into it. That is when we found out that I couldn't move. Anything.

> Psalm 69:1-3 Save me, O God! For the waters have come up to my neck. I sink in deep mire, where there is no standing; I have come into deep waters, where the floods overflow me. I am weary with my crying; my throat is dry; my eyes fail while I wait for my God.

After a quick trip back into the Emergency Room, where they tried to determine the extent of my problem, it was back into the decompression chamber for another seven hours! Seven hours of fighting back spasms, struggling to suck air into my lungs, and being constantly prodded and probed. In my torment I lifted my heart to the Lord. "Oh Jesus," I prayed, "please be with me through this. Help me, Lord, and get me through this trial."

Wouldn't it be wonderful to say that after this prayer God sent an angel to sit with me in the chamber and take away my pain and paralysis? Well, God doesn't often work that way. However in John 14 Jesus promises *and I will pray the Father, and He will give you another Comforter, that He may abide with you forever.* A comforter. A paraclete. The Holy Spirit. I cried unto the Lord, and He did not take away my pain and paralysis, but sent the Holy Spirit to help me bear it. Praise God!

After the operators pulled me out of the chamber this time, it was back to the Emergency Room. There they poked and prodded, and we finally came to a rather chilling conclusion...the chamber hadn't worked. I couldn't move from the chest down. I had no feeling from the chest down. I was paralyzed! I was a quadriplegic!

It was now very early in the morning, and I was wheeled up to the Neurological Intensive Care Unit (NICU) where I was admitted. But Jesus was still with me. Amazingly, I wasn't worried about the fact that I couldn't move anything! I wasn't dismayed by the fact that I was facing a very uncertain future. But I was concerned about the worry that I was going to be to my wife, Chris.

When Chris came the next morning, expecting to pick me up and take me home, I was back in the chamber. She peeked in the porthole at me, and kept a happy face on...but she had to be aching inside. We had just had our twenty-fourth anniversary in June, and during all that time the only time either of us was in the hospital was for the delivery of our two kids. Now she wasn't sure what to do. How long would I be in the hospital, and what was this going to do to our transfer to Maryland? How about the house? We were renting it back from the family who had purchased it, and they were scheduled to take possession in two weeks! Where could Chris and the kids live? What about the house we had bought in Maryland? What were we going to do?

When I got back to my room in the NICU, and Chris came in, all I could do was cling to her and cry. I was so sorry for what I was putting her through. I didn't feel any worry for myself, but I had always been the "macho take care of the family" type of husband. Not that I didn't think that Chris was capable. When I was in Viet Nam she had handled things well, and when I was a salesman in the furniture industry she was the one that handled all the bills and books. I knew she could do it. I just didn't want her to *have* to. That was my job.

Proverbs 19:14 says, in part, *a prudent wife is from the Lord.*

As I sobbed my apology to Chris she quietly and firmly reminded me that our marriage vows had said that she was marrying me "for better or for worse," and that we would weather this storm together. The dictionary defines "prudent" as wise, considerate, thoughtful. My Chris was definitely "from the Lord." She would show her resolve and strength over and over again as the weeks and months and, now years of this trial wore on.

Two days after my accident the doctors decided that they wanted to perform a series of MRIs on me to try to determine if there was any structural neurological damage done, and if they could find some reason why the accident happened. At that time, for an MRI you were loaded onto a narrow stretcher and slid into a tiny cylinder where you did not even have enough room to reach up and scratch your nose. Your arms were pinned at your sides, the top of the tube was two inches away from your nose, and you were totally immobile. My back was still strained at this time, and lying on this hard stretcher started it spasming again. I was in discomfort. I was not claustrophobic, but between the pain and the confinement I started to lose control. Then I remembered Jesus had promised that He would be with me always. Again I called to Him for help. I prayed and I recited scripture verses and I sang favorite hymns in my mind. I wasn't entirely in my proper mind, I guess, and apparently some of my prayers weren't just between the Lord and me. The attendant heard me and called down into the tube to make sure that I was all right. I wasn't, but I assured him that there wasn't anything that Jesus and I couldn't get through together. I don't know how long an MRI takes, but it seemed like forever...until I started turning it over to God. Then I lost myself in my prayers and praise, and soon it was over.

I don't know whether you have spent any time in a hospital room. I hope not. But if you have, you know what a drab and (you should forgive the pun) "lifeless" place it can be. Mercy Hospital being a Catholic hospital, at least I had the comfort of a crucifix on the wall, but otherwise it was rather bleak. When it was known that I was being admitted my family started bringing in little inspirational plaques and other things to keep me company. One favorite item was a little white stuffed toy bunny with a bandage on his ear that said "Get Well Soon." He still sits in an honored spot on top of my computer as a reminder of my daughter's love for me. These little things started to brighten up my room. And then the get-well cards started coming.

Psalm 23:6 Surely goodness and mercy shall follow you all the days of your life.

When I was being charged and blessed at a graduation ceremony from a spiritual warfare school this passage was given to a pastor's wife for me. She interpreted it to mean that as many things as I liked to do for others, I often felt that my actions went unappreciated, but that those for whom I did them did recognize my actions, did appreciate them, and that I was loved. Well, I did feel that way, occasionally, that people didn't appreciate the things that I tried to do for them, and it was a comfort to have Marion tell me this.

Then the get-well cards started coming. Not just a few. Actually, not just a lot. A ton! They came from co-workers and churches. They came from people who did not know me personally, but whom I had touched indirectly in some way. They came from family and friends. There were tiny ones, and two huge cards must have had over 100 signatures on each of them! My family taped these cards to the wall of my room, and soon it was colorful and joyful. And the love that they expressed! Even now it causes tears to come to my eyes as I think about it. And the prayers that they sent and promised! God must have gotten sick of hearing my name from so many places. Ultimately I had over 250 cards, banners and posters taped to the walls of my hospital room, and prayer chains from Key West to Connecticut to California praying for me. *"Surely goodness and mercy shall follow me all the days of my life."* My Lord, I did not know that so many people even knew of me, much less thought so much of me. It was and is simply overwhelming!

> In *1 Thessalonians 5:16-18* the Apostle Paul writes, *Rejoice always, pray without ceasing, in everything give thanks; for this is the will of God in Christ Jesus for you.*

Jesus stood with me in this trial. I never had any doubt about why this accident had happened…it was because the Lord has something planned for me. Rather than being depressed and lying in bed asking, "Why me," I was lying there saying, "OK, Lord. You've got my attention. What have you got planned for me?" Even in the times of pain I was actually able to pray my thanks to God for the lessons in humility that He was giving me. I didn't know why this all was happening, but I put my trust in God. I thanked Him for everything that was taking place, and that helped buoy my spirits throughout my ordeal.

They kept me in the NICU at Mercy Hospital for two weeks. My paralysis was so complete that they were afraid that it would spread upwards and affect my diaphragm, causing me to stop breathing. They wanted me wired to all of the monitoring equipment so that they could react quickly should it be necessary to intubate me. During that time I was going into the hyperbaric chamber twice a day for three hours at a time. I was also receiving some occupational and physical therapy in my room. The Physical Therapists (PTs) kept trying to get me up into a standing position or into a wheelchair to take me to the physical therapy gym, but I had no control over my legs, and I kept ending up on the floor. I knew that my young therapists were trying to do the right thing, but they apparently did not understand the degree of my paralysis. Nor the fact of my size. At 6'3" and 230 pounds, it was going to take more than a 110-pound young woman to get me standing. On two occasions they managed to slide me from my bed in the NICU into a wheelchair, bruising me pretty well on the way, then, when they brought me back, they couldn't figure out how to get me back into the bed. So they would transfer me into a recliner chair, and leave me there for the men from the hyperbaric chamber to figure out. It was not one of the better parts of my hospital stay. One positive aspect of this treatment, though, was the attention that it got me from my NICU nurses. Those angels took personal charge of, and interest in, their patients, and when the rehab folks would drop me, or someone else would bring me back just totally wiped out from testing and hyperbaric treatments, these nurses would be there immediately to try to get me cleaned up, comfortable, rested, and just cared for. They got real ticked off when they finally managed to get me feeling halfway human, only to have someone else come in and wear me down to a nub again.

The one thing that made my morning trips into the hyperbaric chamber easier was looking forward to getting out and seeing Chris. She would keep in contact with the chamber, knowing about when I was due to go in, and would time her departure from home for the hospital so that she would be there when I got out. Often she would call while I was in the chamber, and the people on the outside would relay messages in to me. Almost every day they would pass the message, "Chris said to tell you she's leaving for the hospital, now." It gave me a time frame—something on which to base the rest of my morning in the chamber.

Twenty-four years before this I had been married to Chris when I went off to basic training in the Army. I often told people, then, that the knowledge that she was there waiting for me made all the hassles of basic training easier to take. I knew that I had an anchor on the outside, and it gave me strength.

Again, when I went as a soldier to the Republic of Viet Nam, knowing that Chris was at home, thinking of me and loving me and missing me kept me going. She was my light at the end of the tunnel, and her love and constancy kept me going through the wartime separation.

Now, once more, Chris was my anchor back in the "real world." Every day she would drive the forty-five minutes from our home down to Mercy Hospital to be with me when I got out of the chamber. Much of the time once I got back to my room I was so worn out that I would drift in and out of sleep while she sat there and watched me, but the times when I was awake, and Chris would lean over my bed and let me hug her and smell her and feel her love…those were little bits of paradise there in my little hospital room. I can't begin to express the feelings of love and comfort that those times brought to me.

At the end of two weeks in the Mercy Hospital NICU, and twenty sessions in the hyperbaric chamber, they decided that it was time to get me into an intensive rehab program, and I was transferred to South Miami Hospital. Poor Chris! Now she had ten miles further to drive to come and visit me! Until Hurricane Andrew hit, however, she still didn't miss a day. Throughout all this, Chris has told me, she just relied on Philippians 4:19 as her motto, *My God will supply all your needs according to his glorious riches in Christ Jesus.* She trusted in God to keep her going. Praise the Lord! He did just that. Through it all, God never failed her, and she never failed me.

My life in South Miami Hospital was a different story. For one thing, at South Miami I had two Christian nurses. One of them was a little tentative about broaching the Christianity topic with a patient. She was working on me, and said something about religion, but quickly added that she wasn't allowed to talk religion with the patients because she could get into trouble. I quickly informed her that if she were going to come into MY room, she would have to talk religion. That broke the ice, and we formed a close bond of Christian love. She loved her job, as a nurse, but not just because it made her feel good to help people. It was because…gosh. How do I say it? I guess the easiest thing to say is that you could and can see Jesus shining out from her eyes when she is helping her patients. It's not just a job or a profession, it is a Christian calling. And even if she is not allowed to TALK about Jesus, she definitely lets people SEE Jesus in her.

But *my* main job at South Miami was downstairs in rehab. There, too, I was blessed with having a Christian PT that occasionally worked with me, and a Christian occupational therapist full-time.

For those of you who don't know, occupational therapy deals with restoring your upper body strength and your manual dexterity. By this time I had regained a fair amount of use of my arms and hands, though my fingers were still numb, and the least bit of exercise had me huffing and puffing and soaked with sweat. But OT wasn't too bad. Over in physical therapy…that is where the real work was. That was where I had to learn to walk again.

We started on July 26th. The PT wanted to see how well I could stand. Here we go again! So she wheeled me over to the parallel bars, and between the therapist and me and the bars I stood, sort of, for a few seconds. But it was something of a disappointment. It was *so* hard! Then the therapist decided to get me out of my chair and onto a "mat," which was really a large table a few feet off the floor, to evaluate me a little further. You guessed it. You remember I told you about my legs not working when people tried to move me? Well, it happened again. She tried to lift me, and I headed south. Actually, I learned something interesting about medical semantics. If you don't actually hit the floor, they don't call it dropping. All in all, I "wasn't dropped" five times during my time in the hospital.

But they knew what they were doing at South Miami. They pushed me and I pushed them, and together we worked my numb and lifeless arms and legs trying to wake something up…trying to bypass the non-responding nerves and create new channels for the impulses to travel.

Philippians 4:13 reads, *I can do all things through Christ who strengthens me.*

On the 4th of August I stood in the parallel bars and the therapist pulled my legs forward, one at a time, as I "walked" the length of the bars—my first steps since my accident in July. I wasn't satisfied with the therapist moving my legs for me, though, so the next day I went back to physical therapy, and after my various exercises, I stood between the parallel bars, and I moved my own legs as I walked to the end of the bars, turned around, walked back and collapsed into my wheelchair soaked in sweat from the exertion. *I can do all things through Christ who strengthens me.* To God be the glory! I was walking! And I kept on pushing and working. They warned me that I would learn to hate my therapists as they pushed me to perform, but I ended up pushing them to push me further. On August 7th, just three days after my first therapist-assisted steps, I managed to get up from my wheelchair and shuffle a few hesitant steps with a walker.

> *James 5:15-16 And the prayer of faith will save the sick, and the Lord will raise him up…pray for one another, that you may be healed. The effective fervent prayer of a righteous man avails much."*

I had prayer chains working on me from Key West to Connecticut to California, and on September 15th, I walked out South Miami Hospital, and rode home with Chris.

You ask if I stayed positive and happy through my entire ordeal in the hospital. No. God blesses me, but I'm still human. Things still got to me. In Mercy Hospital, after about a week and a half I was beginning to get some strength and use back in my right hand. It gave me a feeling of success and a major step back toward normalcy. Then the nurse changed my IV from my left and useless hand into my right hand. I could no longer use it. I asked her not to do it, but she didn't listen. I suddenly had lost what little gain I had made and it threw me into about a day and a half of deep depression.

Then there was the time in South Miami. It was early September, I had been in the hospital almost two months, I had been thinking that I should take Chris away, somewhere, when I got out. Maybe we could go to the Gulf Coast to the beach. We could walk in the sand and…no, wait a minute. I can't walk in the sand. Well, maybe we can go to a really nice motel that has pools and hot tubs, and we can…no, I can neither get down into nor up out of a hot tub. Come to think of it, I can't even get into a bathtub. I need a shower stall with a chair in it and grab bars so that I don't fall. And all of a sudden it hit me…I'M DISABLED! I don't think that I got as depressed about being disabled as sobered by the realization that things had changed. A lot. Now Chris and I would have to view things through a new reality.

But as long as that new reality is based around my belief in Jesus Christ and His power in my life, how can we possibly go wrong?

Why was God so good to me in my healing? Was it because someone had told Him about me? No, although there were enough prayer chains working on my behalf to give God a headache. Was it because I knew *about* Him? No. Even the demons know *about* Him. It was and is because I *KNOW* Him. Personally. I have a Friend whom I talk to on a daily basis. His name is Jesus Christ. He's my friend, and when this happened to me, He was right there with me. I talked the problem over with Him, and He said, "Dave, don't worry about it. I'll talk with My Father about it, and We'll get it taken care of."

So, beloved, that is why I am able to walk today…to be able to stand and tell people my story. I've had some people call me a "hero." No. I'm not a hero. Chuck Colson has said that a hero is someone who does something that he doesn't have to. I did what the Lord told me to do. That's not heroic. That's only trying to be obedient to God's will and direction. And He blesses it.

No, I've not been completely healed. Not physically. Paul had his "thorn in the side," and I have my continuing paralysis, but I am able to continue to cope with it because I know that the Lord allowed it to happen. No, I still don't know what the Lord has planned for me. I thought that He had allowed this to happen so that I could retire early from the Coast Guard and move into a pulpit. I've not found a pulpit to accept me. I thought that with prayer He'd quickly let me know what He had in mind for me. God's time is not our time. He's not yet ready to tell me what He has planned for me. I've always been the extensive planner and organizer. In spiritual gifts surveys Administration is always one of my gifts, along with Exhortation, Teaching and

Mercies. In the Coast Guard I was the one called on to unravel the messes and problems. I guess that He is teaching me more patience and letting me know that He is in charge. He'll do the planning, and He will tell me when and what. He has *something* planned for me, and He has a *time* when He is going to want me to do it. I just have to wait, patient in the love and grace that He showers down on me, basking in His warmth and appreciating the fruits of His work. "Someday Jesus will call my name," says the popular song. "Hear I am, Lord," say both scripture and the popular hymn. And until the call comes, I just continue to read and pray and luxuriate in His loving kindness. Praise Him!

If you don't have that kind of personal relationship with Jesus, I'd like to introduce the two of you right now. He died just to be able to know you. So if you don't know Him, and if you'd like to get a really close relationship set up with Him, how about bowing your head with me just now while we introduce ourselves. All you need to do is pray a simple little prayer, and mean it in your heart, and my good friend Jesus will become your good friend Jesus. Will you pray that prayer? Just bow your head and say: *"Oh, Jesus, I'm a sinner. I know that I am, and I know that my sin has kept me apart from you and from God. But I am sorry for my sin, and I want us to be friends. So please, Jesus, come into my heart right now. I want to go further than just to know about you, I want to know you…as my personal friend…as my personal savior. Thank You, Jesus. Praise You, Jesus. Amen."* If you prayed that prayer, we're now family. You, me, a whole huge bunch of wonderful people, and Jesus Christ. Hi there, Brother! It's certainly good to see you. Welcome to the family!

APPENDIX B

An Easter Musing

For my beloved Jewish friends, I wish you a Happy Passover. May Elijah visit your Seder. For those of you who are into New Age, I wish you...whatever.

But this is Holy Week, for us Christians, the most wonderful time of the year, and I have here a look at the crucifixion of Jesus that I have adapted from a number of sources including the Via de Cristo, Walk to Emmaus, Mike Warnke, and my own research.

THE CRUCIFIXION

The Scriptures refer to the actual physical punishment of Jesus in almost a cursory fashion. In John 19:1 we read "Pilate then took Jesus and had him scourged," and Luke 23:33 says, "And when they came to the place called *The Skull*, they crucified him there, and the robbers, one on his right hand and the other on his left." So few words to describe what Jesus experienced.

During Holy Week Christians are joyous, and so we should be. It is the time when we commemorate the fact of resurrection and the salvation that it brings to us. Jesus died for our sins, and for that we rejoice. We are sadly remiss, however, if we do not consider just how terribly Jesus *suffered* for us. Remember: he became man so that he could live and die in remission of our sins. He did not rise above suffering; he accepted it *for us*, yet we seem to acknowledge it almost as nonchalantly as the Bible seems to record it. We should, we *must*, consider just what Jesus endured for us.

What did take place? They arrested Jesus at night, while He was in prayer. The Pharisees were jealous and frightened of Him. The people loved Him, and the Pharisees were afraid of losing their power, so they trumped up a bunch of false charges against Him, and held a mockery of a trial. They wanted to totally do away with Him, to erase Jesus from the scene, but the Jewish law did not allow them to execute Him. So after their trial they hauled Jesus back and forth through the streets of Jerusalem, from one Roman official to another until they finally convinced Pontius Pilate to take some action. Pilate was afraid that if he didn't do something to placate these hotheads they would cause trouble, and he'd get in trouble with Rome for not keeping the peace. So to try to keep the people at rest, Pilate decided to give in and give a little punishment to Jesus. He'd been accused of treason and He'd been accused of blasphemy so the Roman governor took Jesus out and had Him scourged. That should be enough to satisfy anybody.

"Scourged." Visualize this, now: They tied Jesus like a criminal, and they dragged Him out to a place called the Court of the Pavements. In the middle of the Court of the Pavements there was a post, about three feet high, and at the top of the post there was an iron ring. This was the scourging post. They forced Jesus into a kneeling position, took the rope that tied Jesus' hands together, and they put the end of the rope through the ring at the top of the post. They wanted Him kneeling so that when they whipped him, the whip would wrap around his entire body. They pulled on the rope until they had Jesus stretched out. They tied the rope off, stepped back, and ripped Jesus' robe off of His back. They saw that His skin was nice and tight so that when the whip hit Him it would be sure to rip and tear. Then they brought the scourges out.

There was no more diabolical instrument of torture in those days. The scourge, the Roman *flagrum*, was a whip with one handle, and three leather tongues. At the tip of each tongue of the scourge was a piece of metal shaped like a barbell. It is said that some of the barbells had a claw-like protrusion to ensure maximum damage to the victim.

To make certain that each lash was applied with maximum force, there were two men with scourges who would alternate blows. These guys were the ones who were in charge of the disciplinary actions taken against the entire Roman legion in Jerusalem. They were huge muscled men who had flogged hundreds of Roman legionnaires, and they had an attitude. They felt that they had done their best for Rome, but here they were, stuck in one of the worst assignments of all. Judea was considered almost a punishment tour. It was far from home, the people were hateful, the climate was nasty, and the customs were really strange. This was a chance for them to take out some of their animosity and frustration against a leader of these Jews. So they walked up to this task with real relish.

The men stood on opposite sides of Jesus, took their whips and shook them out. Sometimes a really ambitious Sergeant-at-arms would coat the length of the three tongues of his whip with sheep's blood, and stick broken shards of pottery to it for more damage. The first man looked at Jesus' back, with the skin stretched tight, measured his distance, and with his big muscled arm he brought that whip whistling down on Jesus' back. Now the reason for the kneeling position was obvious. In addition to allowing gravity to accelerate the blow, the bent-forward kneeling position allowed the tongues of the scourge to wrap themselves around Jesus' body, and cut into Him. The pieces of metal clawed at Him. The bits of broken pottery cut into his flesh. When the man had a good bite on Jesus, he would twist the whip and pull it away so that hunks of flesh would be ripped off of Jesus' body. The first strokes of the scourging would cut the surface skin, while the lead balls would cause deep bruises. Later strokes would cut deep, causing venous and arterial bleeding, and opening the bruises so that they bled too. Jesus took 39 stripes like that. 39 times those arms rose up and fell. 39 times that whip bit into Jesus—front and back, from the top of his shoulders to the top of his legs. By the end of the scourging the flesh literally hung off of Jesus' back in tattered strips. Josephus, the Jewish historian, said that Jesus Christ was reduced to human rubble.

The histories of the day say there was not one inch on Jesus' body that wasn't cut or bruised or bleeding or gashed open. Jesus took 39 lashes like that.

Then they cut Him down, and Jesus slumped to the pavement, too weak from shock and loss of blood to stand. The Sergeants-at-arms gave the rest of the legionnaires a chance to take out some of their frustrations. Someone had called Him the king of the Jews, so one of the legionnaires went and got a purple robe. They flung it over Jesus' battered body. Then they did something that was new for the Romans, and was never done again. The Bible says that they made a crown of thorns, but it would not have been possible for them actually to plait a crown out of the indigenous thorns without badly scratching themselves. St. Vincent of Lrins wrote: "The placed on His head a crown of thorns; it was, in the shape of a *pileus*, so that it touched and covered His head in every part." What the Romans did was cut off a bushy branch from the lote tree, with its inch-long thorns, and crush this onto Jesus' head. They beat it down around His ears with rods until the inch-long thorns just stuck into His scalp and gouged into His face. The scalp is one of the thinnest areas of skin on the entire body, so the wounds from the thorns would have had the blood freely running down His face from the puncture wounds.

Then the Roman soldiers put a scepter in His hand...and they mocked Him...and they spit on Him...and they pulled out His beard in fistfuls...and they called Him a king...and they laughed at Him. The Bible says they smote Him in the face. The Greek word that they use there—to smite—is the same Greek word that they use for striking a man with a closed fist. It is the root word for the word "pugilism," which means boxing. It was striking Jesus full in the face with a closed fist. They beat Jesus with their fists...the whole company of Romans did.

When they finished with that they dragged Jesus back in and gave Him to the procurator, Pilate, and Pilate brought Him out to the crowd. This was the same crowd that a week before had hailed Jesus as the Messiah. Just one week before they had spread palms and their cloaks on the road before Him and cried "Hosanna!" as He rode into the holy city. They had said that they'd love Him, and follow Him and stick by Him forever. Pilate stood Jesus before this crowd, and next to Him he stood a murderer named Barabbas. Pilate told the crowd, "I'll give you either one of these men you want. I'll give you this murderer, Barabbas, or I'll give you this man, here, in whom I can find no fault. I'll give you Jesus, who is supposed to be your king. Now which do you want?" And on top of the scourging, on top of the humiliation, on top of the pain and the loss of blood, Jesus had to stand there and watch the people He loved turn their backs on Him and scream for the release of Barabbas. He had to stand there and watch while everybody He cared for deserted him, and He had to stand there and listen to the shouts of "Give us Barabbas. We want Barabbas. Crucify Jesus. Crucify Him…we want Barabbas."

Pilate feared the crowd, so he agreed to have Jesus crucified.

They took Jesus out, and it says that they ripped the purple robe off of His back. In order to do that they would have had to rip off the crown of thorns, first, tearing open new wounds in His scalp. Then the robe. The wounds on His back had had a chance to congeal with the blood, and tearing off the robe ripped every one of them open again, and again He began to bleed profusely from the wounds of the scourge.

The soldiers then placed the 120-pound horizontal beam of the cross, the *patibulum*, on Jesus' shoulders and tied His outstretched arms to it, and they made Him walk up the Via Dolorosa. The Way of Sorrows, it is called now, but it is the street in Jerusalem that is probably the steepest. As He started making His way up the street He was weak. He had been severely beaten, He was deserted, His disciples weren't even in the area, and He fell. It was too much. The strain and the loss of blood…Jesus fell under His cross. Three times Jesus fell with the cross lashed across His shoulders. His body was bare, and the street was stone, so each time He fell He lacerated His knees. The cross weighed so much, and He was so weak, that each time He fell his face would be slammed into the street, also. After the third fall a man stepped out of the crowd, a man called Simon of Cyrene. The Bible doesn't say what nationality he was, but tradition says that he was a black man. This man came out and picked up the cross. He took it up for Jesus and carried it the rest of the way to Golgotha…the place of the skull.

They put the beam down on the ground, and threw Jesus down naked on it. They stretched His arms out, and got a square iron spike. The spike was over ¼" thick with a large flat head on it to keep the impaled wrist from slipping off of it. They took Jesus' hand, placed it against the wood of the cross, and put that spike in the lower part of His wrist, where the small bones are. They put a foot on Jesus' palm, put the nail down in the heel of His hand, took a heavy mallet…and they drove that nail through His hand, through His flesh and bones, and into the wood of the cross. Then they stretched out His other hand, and did the same. When the spike pierced Jesus' wrist it would lacerate the median nerve. Doctors say that just touching this nerve causes great excruciating pain, but Jesus had nails driven through His.

Then they lifted Jesus up, nailed to the crossbeam, and dropped the crossbeam onto a peg in the upright of the cross. This violent drop, too, would have torn at the median nerve, adding more crushing pain for Jesus.

Then they took Jesus' feet. They took one foot, placed it on top of the other, instep to sole, slightly bent Jesus' knees, and took another of the large-headed iron spikes. They put the spike the middle of His top instep, drove it through both feet, and out through His back heel into the cross. Jesus was nailed to the wood of the cross.

Crucifixion was and is the most horrible way to die ever devised by man. As Jesus hung on His hands, in His weakened condition, the agony was such that it ran down His arms and into His chest. It caused massive diaphragm spasms, and pinched off His lungs so that He couldn't breathe. The only way that Jesus could get any relief was to push all of His weight up on the nail in His feet and stand upright to gasp a couple of breaths of air.

It was during those times that He pushed Himself upright to gasp for air that He said such things as: "Father, forgive them, for they know not what they do."

It wasn't just for the Roman soldiers that He said that. He was looking all the way down through history, and He was looking right at you and right at me. He was looking at every one of us that He was hanging on that cross for. He wasn't just hanging on that cross for the previous sins of the world, or even for the sins of the world that He lived in. He was hanging on the cross for your sins and my sins too.

Crucifixion was such a diabolical torture. The crucified could live, in untold agony, for up to three days. But on that Friday Jesus pushed Himself up for one last time. He said: "It is finished." His head fell forward on His chest, He slumped back down on His arms for the last time, and He died. He lived for three hours on the cross, and when He died, He chose the time and the hour and place of His death, because when He died He gave His spirit up. Jesus' mother and His brothers came, and they took Him down, and they put Him in a borrowed tomb because the Lord of Glory couldn't even afford a grave of His own. They put Him in that place, and they rolled a stone in front of it. They took wax and sealed the tomb with the great seal of Rome, and they posted a Roman guard saying "anyone who breaks this seal, put them to death immediately." The Pharisees knew the stories, and they didn't want anyone to steal Jesus' body and claim that He had risen from the dead.

With the coming of the night came the gloating of Satan. He had been fighting with God ever since Genesis 3:15, and now believed that he had won. Jesus, God incarnate, was in the tomb, and Satan was celebratory.

Satan turned to his two lieutenants, Death and Corruption, and said: "Death, I got that Jew Jesus, in a hole in the ground. And He's really dead. I want you to make sure He stays that way. I want you to wrap yourself around Him, and I want you to hold on to Him like you never held onto anybody before."

Death said, "Well, anybody I've ever got my bony fingers on I've still got."

The devil turned to Corruption, and said, "OK, now, Death is going to hold Him. I want you to just dissolve Him to dirt and blow Him away...I don't want to have any traces of Jesus left."

Corruption said, "Anyone Death can hold I can rot."

It was three days later that Satan heard from Death and Corruption.

Death said, "I really tried to hold Jesus, but there was something about Him...I just couldn't hold Him."

And Corruption said, "Yeah I couldn't even touch Him. Not only could I not put corruption on Him, I couldn't even touch Him!"

In fear Satan looked down one of the long, dark corridors of Hell...and there, way down at the bottom of The Pit, for the first time ever there was a little glimmer of light. And that light shone out bright, in the pit, and it started coming toward the devil and Death and Corruption. As it came forward it got bigger and brighter, and bigger and brighter, and every time one of these beams of light would hit one of the cell doors, where the spirits of the people were kept, the cell door would just pop open! The people would come out of their cells praising God and singing, Hosanna! Hallelujah! They'd be praising the name of the Lord, and everything in Hell was in chaos. People were running free, Hell was all lit up, and the Satan was shaking all over. And the devil looked way down in the deep part of that light, where it was coming from, and guess who it was? It was Jesus, striding through the corridors of Hell. It wasn't the beaten, crucified Jew of the cross, but it was the risen, glorified Lord of Glory, who's called Wonderful, Counselor, the Mighty God, the Everlasting Father, the Prince of Peace.

And Jesus came striding through the corridors of Hell, and all the people were with Him singing and praising God. Jesus walked right up to Death and Corruption and the devil. He grabbed Death and threw him off this way. He grabbed Corruption and threw him off that way, and he reached out and grabbed Satan, shook him real hard three times, and said, "Hand over those keys!"

So the devil went down and got out the keys, and went through the A's and B's and C's until he got down to the J's, and it said **Jesus of Nazareth** on it. Jesus took it, and looked at it, and said, "You know, that's pretty good. But I can see into the future. I know that you can't see into the future, Satan, because if you could you would have known that getting crucified was just what We had planned. And if you could see into the future you could see way down there, way down to May 15, 1988, to Cooper City, Florida, and there's a guy named David Wilson, and he is going to need his key. So while I'm here, devil, why don't you just give me Dave Wilson's key, too? As a matter of fact, as I see into the future I see that there are a lot of people who are going to need their keys. So, while I'm here, I'll just take them all."

And Jesus took the keys of Death, Hell and the grave away from Satan. He shoved Satan aside. He went up and put His hand in the middle of the gates of Hell, and pushed them open! He pushed them open for you and for me. And the Son rose on the third day.

Happy Resurrection Day!

About the Author

David Thatcher Wilson is a disabled veteran who served with the 101st Airborne Division in Viet Nam, and retired from the U.S. Coast Guard. He is an adjunct professor at Trinity International University and Florida International University, in Miami, and his weekly e.letter **Sunday Musings** is a regular feature in ***Christian Churches Monthly***. He lives, with his wife, Chris, in Ft. Lauderdale and on Virginia's Eastern Shore.

0-595-25829-8